D1269205

A LITERARY HISTORY OF WALLPAPER

1 An example of John Baptist Jackson's work in Chiaro-Oscuro, giving, by means of overprinting, some ten shades from four oil colours. Date about 1750. (See *An Essay on the Invention of Engraving and Printing in Chiaro-Oscuro* 1754)

A Literary History of WALLPAPER

E. A. ENTWISLE

"*Each age, each kindred, adds a verse to it*"
LOWELL, *Bibliolatres*, St. 6

LONDON
B. T. BATSFORD LTD

First published 1960

MADE AND PRINTED IN GREAT BRITAIN BY
WILLIAM CLOWES AND SONS, LIMITED, LONDON AND BECCLES
FOR THE PUBLISHERS
B. T. BATSFORD LTD
4 Fitzhardinge Street, Portman Square, London, W.1.

PREFACE

The idea of this book came to me in 1945 when I was asked to compile a 'bibliography' of wallpaper for the Catalogue of the Wallpaper Exhibition which was held at the Suffolk Galleries in May of that year. Up to that time I had never listed systematically the many books on wallpaper to which I had often referred during a lifetime's interest in the subject and the 'bibliography', when it made its appearance, was inaccurately described as such and far from being a comprehensive list; but it was a start, at least, and in the years which followed I was able to make innumerable additions until at last it became full enough to be interesting and even useful to those who appreciated, and who wished to know more about, the important role which wallpaper has always played in interior decoration. This is not to say that the references which follow are considered to be complete or even fully representative: on the contrary such a work as this can never reach finality, for every year that passes brings some new contribution to the literature of wallpaper and new discoveries in past publications are always being made. Indeed it is my earnest hope that this book, because of its very limitations, will encourage readers to add their own references to the list and so make subsequent editions, if any, more comprehensive.

As will be seen the quotations really begin during the 17th century but it should be remembered that at this period wallpaper had not yet attained the acceptance or popularity which it achieved during the succeeding century. In 1509, for instance, the year in which the so-called earliest wallpaper was printed, people were still using wall coverings of the most rudimentary or luxurious types, such as wool or serge, painted or plain, or excessively sumptuous silks, tapestries, wood panelling and decorated leathers; the latter being the immediate forerunners of wallpaper. In fact it was not until about 1700 that wallpaper reached a scale of commercial production sufficient to enable John Houghton, in 1699, to recommend it as being worthy of general encouragement (p. 13).

As interest in wallpaper grew, so it became an ever increasing source of informed comment, eventually taking its place in the early encyclopaedias and dictionaries, many references to which are included in the pages which follow. Wallpaper was invariably admired by polite society and those who, travelling widely, were moved to record what they saw in detail. The wealth of information available from these sources is demonstrated in the number of quotations recorded and this aspect of the notes is by no means least important. We are brought very closely in touch with a past age when we read the intimate views of those who lived in it; and when, as is often the case, letters and memoirs contain a detailed description of a new wallpaper just put up, the reference has both charm and significance for this reason.

In this book I have not attempted to deal at length with the many forms of mural decoration which preceded wallpaper though I have mentioned a few of the most authoritative works relating to them under the dates of publication. Papermaking, Tapestry, Mural Painting, Painted Cloths, Decorated Papers and Leather Hangings are touched upon in this way but readers, in such cases, will have to further their own enquiries into all these subjects each of which has a voluminous bibliography of its own. For example, I have omitted Mrs. Celia Fiennes' 17th-century journal in my list because although she describes the tapestry she saw in Queen Anne's rooms at Windsor, it appears she never saw any paperhangings, or if she did, must have forgotten to mention them; and for the same reason I have not mentioned the tapestries made from feathers which Mrs. Elizabeth Montagu hung in her house near Portman Square during the 1780's.

I hope my butterfly collection of fugitive literary comment will be of interest although like the rest of the book it has little in common with a true bibliography. Contrary to expectation wallpaper is not frequently described in the great works of the novelists and my own reading, from which most of the examples quoted have been gleaned, suggests for example that the French novelists have been on the whole more wallpaper-conscious or more observant than the English. It is difficult to find a more evocative description of wallpaper than Proust's discovery, in "A la Recherche du Temps Perdu" of a floral patterned paper which succeeded only in imprisoning him 'in the heart of a poppy out of which to look at a world quite different from in Paris'. And, of course, de Maupassant's grey wallpaper in *Bel Ami* with its 'ancient and suspicious stains' defying analysis, provides an indispensable background for part of this brilliantly written story of human frailty. I have referred to this aspect of my activities as 'butterfly' collecting and it is not easy to think of a more appropriate term for, unless one holds fast to each specimen as it appears and pins it down for future delectation, it has gone as swiftly and as irrevocably as a butterfly on the wing. I have retained the original French in some cases because the sense and sometimes the beauty of the passage is lost in translating.

As will be seen, very important contributions to the subject of wallpaper have been made in America and on the Continent, particularly in France, Germany and Sweden, but I am very much aware, unfortunately, of my failure to record anything but a fraction of what has been published in these and other countries during past years. This applies particularly to Russia for wherever I came across a reference in Russian I was unable to translate it and, of course, it was impossible for me to check the merits of what had been written. The absence of any standard work in Norway, Italy and even Belgium is surprising considering the esteem which wallpaper enjoys in these countries. Even Germany, with its fine and unique Museum of Wallpaper at Kassel, has until now lagged behind in this respect, but it is believed that work has recently been put in hand for the production of a book comparable with those published within recent years in America, France and Great Britain, and its publication is eagerly awaited.

No attempt has been made here to record everything that has been published about wallpaper in widely read magazines and newspapers, for this would be an impossible task seeing that in the past few years alone the number of articles dealing with the subject, especially in English 'women's magazines', is quite incalculable. Almost all magazines devoted to the home and to its decoration at home and abroad, e.g., *Domus* (Italy), *Interiors* (U.S.A.), *Maison et Jardin* (France), and many others have regularly allotted pages to wallpaper and if some of these publications are not mentioned it is because such a record would have involved an amount of work out of all proportion to its usefulness.

Care has been taken to make the index as accurate and as comprehensive as possible and it is hoped that this will enhance the book's value as a serious work of reference.

I would like, in conclusion, to express my sincere thanks to all those who, by their encouragement, practical assistance and advice have made my pleasant task possible and I earnestly hope that the reader will enjoy referring to this book as much as I have enjoyed compiling it.

E. A. ENTWISLE

London W.1 1960

2 Flock box used by wallpaper makers during the early Victorian era [See 1870, TOMLINSON].

ACKNOWLEDGMENT

The author and publisher wish to acknowledge their indebtedness to the following for permission to reproduce illustrations shown:

The Bodleian Library, Oxford; The British Museum; The Cooper Union Museum, New York; The German Wallpaper Museum, Kassel; The Oxford University Archives; The Victoria and Albert Museum and The Worcester Museum; Nancy McClelland, Inc., New York; Mrs. Olga Hirsch; The Wall Paper Manufacturers Ltd.; Weiner Tapetenfabrik A.G., Vienna; Shand Kydd Ltd.; A. Sanderson & Sons Ltd.; Cole & Son (Wallpapers) Ltd.; Hayward & Son Ltd.; John Line & Sons Ltd.

Where the source is not mentioned in the caption, to:

The Earl of Onslow, Pl. 45; The Duke of Bedford, Pl. 52; Capt. E. G. Fairholme, Pl. 13; Laurence Whistler, R.D.I., Pl. 84; Kelly's Directories, Pl. 53; Armstrong Jones, Pl. 96; Stanley J. Pratt, Col. Pl. 40; Whitstable Council, Kent, Pl. 77; Walter Judd Ltd., Royal Academy Illustrated, Pl. 100.

All other illustrations are from the author's collection.

The Literary History

1509 Earliest known wallpaper. Woodcut design of Italian inspiration printed on the back of a Proclamation of Henry VIII. An account of this discovery, at Christ's College, Cambridge, in 1911, is contained in 'Cambridge Fragments', by CHARLES EDWARD SAYLE, in *The Library*, 3rd series, 1911, 1912. Also 'The Master's Lodgings, Christ's College, Cambridge', A. E. SHIPLEY, *Country Life*, 1916, XL, 409. Variants of these accounts appear in most 'histories' of wallpaper from 1911 on.

1555 Stamped paperhangings first made in Spain and Holland. [See *Haydyn's Dict. of Dates*, 1904].

1568 Trial of Herman Schinkel, printer, Delft. [See Notes and Queries 1856].

1577 TAPESTRY, WILLIAM HARRISON (1534–93) writes in his 'Description of England' (*Holinshed's Chronicle*):

'The walls of our houses on the inner sides in like sort be either hanged with tapestry, arras work, or painted cloths, . . . or else they are ceiled with oak of our own, or wainscot brought hither out of the east countries, whereby the rooms are not a little commended, made warm and much more close than otherwise they would be.'

1596 NASHE. (Satirist). Saffron Walden WKS. (Grosart), III, 42.

Let anie man but find me meate and drinke . . . while I am playing the paperstainer.

1609 PIERRE DE L'ESTOILE. *Memoires.* Writing to a friend: 'J'ai donné à M.D.P. six feuilles de mon papier marbré, beau par excellence.'

1620 Paperhangings of velvet and floss first made. [See *Haydyns Dict. of Dates*, 1904].

1627 SIR FRANCIS BACON. *Natural History.* Reference to Marble Papers.

The Turks have a pretty way of chambletting (chamoletting) paper, . . . they take divers oiled colours and put them severally (in drops) upon water and stir the water lightly.

1630 Le François, Rouen, Reputed to have been making flock hangings at this date.

1634 Patent (May 1). Jerome Lanyer. 'Flocking' on various materials.

Whereas our trusty and well-beloved subject and servant, Jerome Lanyer, hath . . . found out an Art and Misterie by affixinge Wooll, Silke, and other Materialls of divers Cullours uppon Lynnen, Cloath, Silke, Cotten,

Leather and other substances with Oyle, Size and other Ciments to make them useful and serviceable for Hangings and other Occasions which he calleth Londrindiana . . .

KNIGHT's *English Cyclopaedia* of 1860 states:

Jerome Lanyer produced what he called 'tonture de laine'. This was cloth on which a design was drawn in varnish or foot oil. A collection of 'flock' or powdered fragments of woollen, was at hand; different colours in different boxes; the flock was sprinkled on the cloth in a peculiar manner by the finger and thumb and thus an attempt was made to imitate costly tapestries and brocades.

3 Reconstruction of the design of the 16th-century wallpaper discovered at Christ's College, Cambridge

1638 LEATHERHANGINGS. Christopher (London), patents a cheap method of decorating leather for mural hangings. EDWIN FOLEY, *The Book of Decorative Furniture*, 1910–11.

1640 J. MUNSELL (Albany, N.Y.) gives this date as the beginning of wallpaper manufacture. [See his *Chronology of Paper and Papermaking*, 1857].

1666 Calendar of State Papers (Domestic) Charles II, July 20, Whitehall. Printed Proclamation forbidding the import or sale of foreign Blue Paper.

Charles Hildyard having invented a new mode of making it and having received a Patent for his invention thereof for 14 years, on his promise to supply the Kingdom sufficiently and at reasonable rates. [See other Paper-making Patents: *A History of English Wallpaper*, 1926, Chap. 3.]

1680 Advertisement: George Minnikin, Stationer, St. Martins le Grand, '*sells all sorts of colour'd paperhangings*' (Bagford Collection, British Museum). [For further examples of advertisements see below.]

1686 Article 61, of French Law, confirms those of 1586, 1618 and 1649 relating to the Guild of Dominotiers, Tapissiers et Imagiers formed in Paris, 1586. [See further references to Dominotiers below.]

1690 Advertisement. (Bagford Collection, British Museum). Edward Butling, Southwark.

At the old Knave of Clubs, at the Bridge foot in Southwark Liveth Edward Butling who maketh and Selleth all sorts of Hangings for Rooms in Lengths or in Sheets, Frosted or Plain. Also a sort of Paper in Imitation of Irish Stich, of the newest Fashion, and several other sorts, viz, Flock Work, Wainscot, Marble, Damask, Turkey Work . . . etc.

1690 ANTOINE FURETIÈRE. *Dictionnaire Universel contenant tous les mots français et les termes de toutes les Sciences et des Arts*, 3 Vols. (Hague). No mention of paperhangings but references to '*Dominotier, one who makes marbled paper and other paper of all colours and printed with various figures.*'

1692 First English Patent for Paperhangings granted in October of this year to William Bayly.

Whereas William Bayly (Bayley), hath by his industry and his great expense found out and invented a new art or invention for printing all sorts of paper of all kinds of figures and colours whatsoever, with several engines made of brass and such other metals with fire, without any paint or stain which will be useful for hanging on walls of rooms and such like uses . . .

1693 Advertisement. *London Gazette* (August 21). '*At the Warehouse for New-Fashioned Hangings, in Newgate St. are made and sold strong Paper-Hangings . . .*' etc.

1693 JOHN EVELYN'S DIARY (July 13). Reference to Queen Mary's '*China and Indian cabinets, screens and hangings*'. [The latter probably refers to Chinese papers.]

1699 JOHN HOUGHTON, F.R.S., *Collection for Improvement of Husbandry & Trade*, reference to Paperhangings. (B.M. Press Mark 966e, 7–10.) (4 Vols.)*

Extracts:

No. 356. May 19, 1699. . . . *Of paper there are divers sorts finer and coarser, as also brown and blue paper, with divers that are printed for the hanging of rooms; and truly, they are very pretty, and make the houses of the more ordinary people look neat. At Ebbisham in Surrey, they call it paper tapestry, and if they be in all parts well pasted close to the wall or boards they are very durable; and it ought to be encouraged, because 'tis introductory to other hangings.*

No. 362. June 30, 1699. *The next in course is Printing which is said to be known in China and other eastern Countries long before it was known in*

* B.M. = British Museum Library

Europe: but their Printing was cutting their Letters upon Blocks in whole pages or Forms, as among us our Wooden Pictures are cut: and a great deal of Paper is nowadays so printed to be pasted upon walls to serve instead of Hangings; and truly if all parts of the sheet be well and close pasted on it is very pretty, clean, and will last with tolerable care a great while; but there are some other done by Rolls in long Sheets of a thick paper made for the Purpose, whose sheets are pasted together to be so long as the Height of a Room; and they are managed like woollen hangings; and there is a great Variety with curious Cuts which are Cheap, and if kept from Wet, very lasting.

1702 Advertisement. *The Postman* No. 1059 (December 10).
At the Blue Paper Warehouse in Aldermanbury (and nowhere else), in London are sold the true sorts of figur'd Paper Hangings, some in pieces of 12 yds long, others after the manner of real Tapestry etc.

1710 Advertisement. Abraham Price (Blue Paper Warehouse). Paperhangings, Wholesale and Retale'. (Gough Collection, Bodleian Library.)

1712 Act: 10 Anne, c. 18, 44. Imposition of Duties on 'paper printed, painted or stained to serve for hangings'.
[See below for variations of this Act.]

1712-13 LADY GRISELL BAILLIE'S *Household Book*, 1692–1733, mentions wallpaper, '*twenty five "pices" stamped paper for £4. 6. 0.*'

1714 Duty as above increased from 1*d.* to 1½*d.* per square yard. (As stated, there were many variations of this duty, but the amount itself, viz., 1½*d.*, remained until 1836 when the duty was repealed.)

1716 Bagford's Collection of Miscellaneous Printed Ephemera. Harleian Collection, B.M. contains Trade Cards, references to Auctions of Wallpaper in the seventeenth century. (Most useful volumes B.M. references 5941, 5942, 5947.)

4 One of a variety of Duty Stamps to be found on the back of many English 18th-century wallpapers

5 Another type of Duty Stamp

6 Fragments of the oldest known wallpaper found *in situ* in 1911 in the Masters Lodge, Christ's College, Cambridge, where it was hung in 1509. See reconstruction of the design on page 12

7 Jacobean wallpaper, *c.*1615, from a box in the Oxford University Archives

8 Fragment of block printed lining paper. English, *c.*1650 (Victoria and Albert Museum)

9 Stuart lining paper from a dower chest. Block printed, black on white

10 Block printed wallpaper of about 1680 revealed by demolition work at Gwernhaylod, near Overton, Flintshire, and discovered by the author in 1952

11 Fragment of English wallpaper; block outline with coloured patches added by hand. *c.*1680–1700

12 Fragment of a late 17th century wallpaper from Brympton D'Evercy, near Yeovil. Black outline with blue, red and green colours added by hand

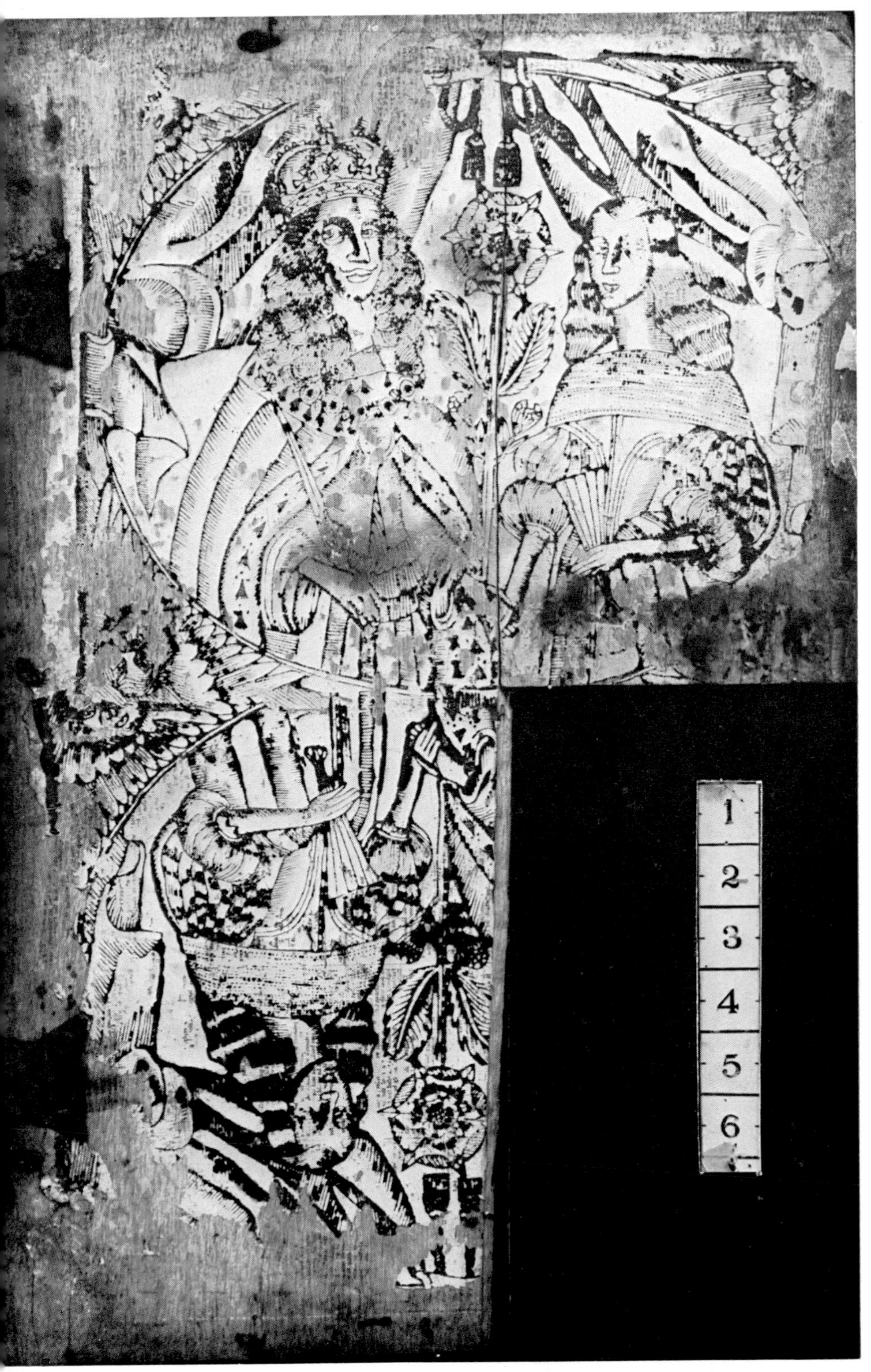

13 Stuart lining paper found in a Bible Box (Charles II and his Queen). Similar pattern discovered in a chest of drawers at Sulgrave Manor, near Banbury. (Illustrated in *The Antiquaries Journal*, 1925)

14 Fragment of flocked leather, *c*.1700, from a house in Friar Street, Worcester. Considered to be an example of the transition from leather to paperhangings. (Worcester Museum)

c.1722 JOHN MACKY. *Journey through England.* Chinese Papers.

Finely adorned with China paper the figures of Men, women, birds and flowers the liveliest (the author) ever saw come from that country. (This is a reference to the Palace of Wanstead).

1723 JACQUES SAVARY DES BRUSLONS. *Dictionnaire Universel de Commerce.* (Geneva.) Contains reference to flock paperhangings. S. de B. was an Inspector of Manufactures. [See 1751 below].

1727 Reference to the use of wallpaper in a Parsonage at St. Columb Major, Cornwall. B.B.C. Talk by W. G. HOSKINS, (See *The Listener*, June 27, 1957.) Exact reference comes from a MS. glebe terrier among the Archdeaconry of Cornwall Records, County Record Office, Truro: '*Two parlours, both floored with boards, one hung with paper, one with plastered walls . . .*', *and*, '*. . . one lodging room (i.e. bedroom) hung with paper.*'

1730 Advertisement. *New England Journal* (October 26). '*John Phillips, Bookseller, sells Stampt Paper in Rolls for to Paper Rooms.*' This and many other wallpaper advertisements from American newspapers listed in *The Arts and Crafts in New England*, 1704–1775, GEORGE FRANCIS DOW, Wayside Press, Massachusetts, 1927.

1734 Bill Head. Robert Dunbar, Aldermanbury, London. Contains instructions for hanging wallpaper:

Please to observe the following Method of putting up the said Hangings in any Room, Viz. First Cut one Edge of each Piece or Breadth, even to the Work, then nail it with large Tacks to the Wall and paste the Edge of the next Breadth over the Heads of the Tacks and so from one to another, till the Room be perfectly hung, observing to make ye Flowers Join. N.B. Damp the Paper before you put it up, and begin next the Window, and make stiff Paste of the best Flour and Water.

1738 *Diary* of JOHN HERVEY, 1st Earl of Bristol.

Paid Thomas Colebrand in full for 20 pieces of paperhangings for Ickworth @ 3/-; £3.

1738 TAPESTRY. *Chambers's Cyclopaedia of Arts & Sciences.* (1st Edn., 1728.) No mention of paperhangings, but under 'Tapestry' there appears the following comment:

Some use (the word) 'Tapestry' as a general name for all kinds of hangings whether woven or wrought with the needle; and whether silken, woollen, linen, leathern, or of paper (in which they are countenanced by the etymology of the word formed from the French: tapisser; to line, Latin: tapes, a cover of a bed, etc.)

[See also 1930: 1957.]

1739 Plunket Fleeson established in Philadelphia the first wallpaper factory in the American Colonies. (*Wall Paper Magazine*, U.S.A., 1952.)

1740 'Robert Dunbar supplies Lord Cardigan with 247 yards of Wallpaper.' [See MCQUOID and EDWARDS, *Dictionary of English Furniture*, London, 1924.]

1740 *The British Merchant*. London periodical Vol. II. References to paper, wallpaper, etc.

1741 Hartford and Pomfret Correspondence.

Lady Hartford is surprised at the perfection the manufacture had arrived at during the last few years and bespeaks a paperhanging.

1743 Trial: *Campbell Craig* v. *Rt. Hon. Richard, Earl of Anglesey*. (Proceedings published 1744.) Contains a reference to printing of wallpapers in Ireland. A witness, one Catharine McCormack, stated that her employment was the printing of papers for the hanging of rooms. She said she worked 'for the best quality in Town'.

1746 KOEPPLIN, *Études sur l'Exposition de 1867*. '*The first wallpaper factories were started in England about this date.*'

1747 *General Description of all Trades* (London). Anonymous. Under 'Papermakers':

There are likewise Hangings for Rooms made by colouring and Embossing of Thick Paper, the making and dealing in which has now become a considerable Branch of Trade. The Masters in this Part seldom take an apprentice with less than £10, at the working Part of which a Journeyman can get 15/- or 18/- a Week, and a Shopman has generally 10, 15, or £20 a year and his Board. To set up in this Branch compleatly will take up £500.

1747 Fanny Boscawen, to her husband, Admiral the Rt. Hon. Edward Boscawen, written from Audley Street, London (December 11). '. . . *my second room is not yet hung, not having been able to get any paper, to my mind, under an exorbitant price. At length, however, I have agreed for one and Bromwich comes to put it up tomorrow.*' [See *Admiral's Wife*, C. A. OGLANDER, 1940. (Bromwich was a well-known London paperhanging maker of the eighteenth century. See CONNOISSEUR, *Bromwich, at the Golden Lyon on Ludgate Hill*, October, 1952)].

1748 A. BENOÎT, 'Tsarkoye Selo.' SPB, 1910, pp. 64 and 150. (Russia) References to the wallpapers in the rooms of the Palace at Tsarkoye Selo at this date.

1749 LADY MARY WORTLEY MONTAGUE writing from Italy (August 22) to her daughter Lady Bute who was then furnishing Caenwood House, states:

I have heard the fame of paperhangings, and had some thoughts of sending for a suit, but was informed that they are as dear as damask here which put an end to my curiosity. (Letters and Works of Lady M. W. Montagu.)

15 Flock wallpaper, *c.*1700. Examples of this particular paper have been found in various parts of the country and can be seen in fig. 20 'Blew Paper Warehouse' advertisement. (*See also* figs. 18, 19)

16 Fragment of early 18th century leather hanging, probably Flemish, discovered in a house in Newport, Monmouth, in 1957

17 Fragments of 18th century decorated paper produced by the firm "Chez les Associe à Paris". Wood block outline, hand coloured in pink, yellow, blue and green. From the collection of Mrs. Olga Hirsch. Size of these fragments 7″ × 4¼″ (approx.)

AT *the Blue-Paper Ware-houſe in Aldermanbury, London,* are Sold the *True Sorts* of *Japan* and *Indian Figured Hangings,* in Pieces of Twelve Yards long, and Half Ell Broad, at 2 *s.* 6 *d.* by the Piece. And another Sort of *Large Japan* and *Foreſt-Work,* in Pieces of proper Sizes, after the new Mode, of Real Tapeſtry. Alſo another Sort, in imitation of Wainſcot, accommodated for Rooms and Stair-Caſes; with great variety of Skreens, Chimney-Pieces, Saſhes, and other things of Curious Figures.

The ſaid Hangings, *&c.* are alſo Sold at the *Japan Ware-houſe* near the *George and Vulture Tavern* in *Cornhil.*

The Patentees for making the ſaid Figur'd Hangings (obſerving the ſame to be counterfeited upon a thin and common Brown Paper, daub'd over with a ſlight and ſuperficial Paint) do hereby give Notice, That the ſaid *True Sorts* may be diſtinguiſh'd from Counterfeits by their Weight, Strength, Thickneſs and Colour, Dy'd through; and are every way more laſting and ſerviceable.

At the ſame Places are to be Sold *Blue Sugar-Loaf* and *Royal purple Paper* by the Ream.

18 Blew or Blue Paper Warehouse, Aldermanbury, London. Advertisement bearing the Arms of William III (1694–1702) and his motto: 'I will maintain'. (Bagford Collection, British Museum)

1749 (December) Mrs. Delany writing to her sister says she has just been to Dufour's, '*The famous man for paper ornaments like stucco.*' *Autobiography and Correspondence of Mrs. Delany.* (Edited, LADY LLANOVER, London, 1861, Vol. II, p. 532.) [See also below.]

1750 MADAME DU BOCAGE, *Letters on England, Holland and Italy*, gives an account of Mrs. Montague's breakfast parties:

In the morning breakfasts agreeably bring together the people of the country . . . in a closet lined with painted paper of Pekin . . .

1750 P. TOYNBEE, *Strawberry Hill Accounts.* 1927. Lady Luxburgh writing to Shenstone (February 13, 1750–1):

Moore, who has lately been at London talks to me of a sort of stucco paper, and says Lord Foley has done his Chapel in Worcestershire, with it, the ceiling at least. By his description the paper is stamped so deep as to project considerably and is very thick and strong . . . etc.

[See 1753 and also 1927, below.]

1751 Mrs. Delany, writing to her brother, '*I have received the 6 doz. borders all safely . . . They are for framing prints.*' (*Autobiography and Correspondence.* See 1749 above.)

1751 MALACHY POSTLETHWAYT'S *Universal Dict. of Trade & Commerce.* [Translation of *Savory des Bruslons Dict.* See above.]

There is also printed, raised, and embossed paper, wherewith to hang rooms, and wherein there is a large consumption, and in which our artists have arrived to great perfection.

1751 DENIS DIDEROT et D'ALEMBERT (JEAN LE ROND). *Encyclopédie ou Dictionnaire Raisonné des Sciences, des Arts et des Métiers* (Paris). Independent articles of considerable interest by J. B. M. Papillon. 1751–1765. Folio. [See 1765].

1752 *Gentleman's Magazine* (February), Vol. XXII, p. 78–79, Remarks on the Art of Printing, Cutting on Wood and Rolling Press Printing.

Mr. Jackson (J. B. J. of Battersea), however, has lately invented a new method of printed paperhangings from blocks, which is very ornamental and exceeds the common method of paperstaining (as it is termed), by the delicacy of his drawings, the novelty of his designs and the masterly arrangment of his principal figures.

1752 EDNA K. DONNELL. *An Enquiry into the Origin of Printing in Europe by a Lover of Art* (London). *Metropolitan Museum Studies*, New York, 1932.

A small booklet the only known copy of which is in the Treasure Room of the Harvard College Library. The author describes J. B. Jackson's method of making paperhangings.

1752 (June 27). *Covent Garden Journal.*

There is scarcely a modern house which has not one or more rooms lined with this furniture . . . (wallpaper).

1752 Advertisement. *London Evening Post.* (April 30–May 2.)

New invented Paperhangings printed in Oyl . . . by J. B. Jackson . .

to be had at Dunbar's Warehouse in Aldermanbury, or at Mr. Gibson's, Bookseller, Charles Street, near St. James's Square, London.

1753 Duke of Bedford decorating Woburn Abbey paid £16 7*s*. '*on account of the China paper*'. (*Family Background*, GLADYS S. THOMPSON, 1949.)

1753 Patent for printing paperhangings granted to Edward Dighton. (Engraved and etched plates of copper and brass passed through a rolling press.)

1753 HORACE WALPOLE to Sir H. Mann (June 12), reference to Strawberry Hill:

The room on the ground floor . . . hung with yellow paper and prints framed in a new manner invented by Lord Cardigan, that is with black and white borders printed.

Further extract: . . . *but in the tower beyond is the charming closet where I am now writing to you. It is hung with green paper and water colour pictures* . . . (There are many references to the Strawberry Hill wallpapers in Horace Walpole's Letters.)

[See also 1927, *Strawberry Hill Accounts.*]

1753 Chambers's Supplement to their *Cyclopaedia*, under 'Papier Maché',

Mr. Boyle tells us that paper, besides its common uses, may be made into frames for pictures, fine embossed work, and other parts of furniture.

[See Ada K. Longfield, 1948. Dossie, 1758, etc.]

1753 Advertisement. *Le Mercure de France*, Vol. II (Juin), Paris.

On trouvera chez le Sieur Prudhomme, Marchand Papetier, Rue des Lombards, vis-à-vis Cinq Diamans, a la Prudence. Un assortiment de feuilles de papiers de la Chine de différentes grandeurs pour tapisseries, dessus de portes, écrans, et paravents . . . etc.

1754 JOHN BAPTIST JACKSON. *An Essay on the Invention of Engraving and Printing in Chiaro Oscuro* (London). (Eight illustrations are included).

Having thus brought this Manner of Engraving on Wood to the Perfection above mentioned, Mr. Jackson has imagined a more extensive way of applying this Invention than has hitherto been thought of by any of his Predecessors; which is the printing Paper for the Hanging of Rooms. . . .

1754 THOMAS CHIPPENDALE. *Gentleman's and Cabinet Maker's Directory* (London). [See 1779 Matthias Darly].

1754 DR. RICHARD POCOCKE mentions seeing at Longford a bedroom '*furnished with Chintz and Indian paper*'. 'Travels through England' etc.

1754 Advertisement. *London Evening Post* (January 8).

The new invented paperhangings infinitely surpass anything of the like nature hitherto made use of, being not distinguishable from rich India paper and the same being beautifully coloured in pencil work and gilt.

1754 Advertisements. *Universal Advertizer*, Dublin (April 6).

Thomas Fuller at the paper-mill on Temple Bar (Ireland), makes the paper called raised stoco [*sic*] *which is as elegant as a real stoco,* . . . etc.

(May 7) Augustin Berville: *the only person who understands the art of making a composition of a particular kind of pasteboard stuccoe, . . .* etc.

1754 Advertisement. *Boston Gazette, U.S.A.* (April 9). William Marchent's '*Printed Paper for Rooms lately imported from London*'.

1754 Mme. de Pompadour had her wardrobe and the passage that led to her apartments hung with English wallpaper.

1755 J. A. ROUQUET, *État des Arts en Angleterre.* Reference to Flock Papers imitating Utrecht velvet. Presumed to contain notes on paperhangings. (B.M. copy destroyed during the war.)

1756 ISAAC WARE. *A Complete Body of Architecture.*

Paper has in great measure taken the place of sculpture . . . and the hand of art is banished from a part of the house in which it used to display itself very happily.

[See 1766, 'London & Westminster Improved'.]

1756 RICHARD ROLT. *A New Dictionary of Trade & Commerce.* [2nd Edition 1761.]

There is likewise another new manufacture of paper brought into England which represents the stuccowork for ornamenting of rooms. [Also brief reference to paperhangings].

1756 Mrs. Delany writing from Cornbury (October 30).

The front room is hung with flowered paper of grotesque pattern; the colours lively, and the pattern bold: the next room with finest Indian paper of flowers and all sorts of birds.

[*Autobiography and Correspondence.* See above.]

1756 *Journal Œconomique.* (Feby). page 92, Reference to French paperhangings.

1756 MOUNSEY. *Phil. Trans. Proceedings of the Royal Society* (Philosophical Transactions) L, 19. '*Mr. Butler, a paperstainer, trying to make some discoveries for the better fixing of colours.*'
[See also 1759.]

1756 *Diary* of MRS. CALDERWOOD, of Polton, Midlothian, reference to her visit to Brussels in September.

The rent of the house in Brussels was only 191 guilders (about £15 a year) and this was furnished, hung with an English flowered paper, all within the space of 10 days.

1757 Advertisement. *Universal Advertizer*, Dublin (March 15). Gordon's Warehouse, at the sign of Hibernia on Temple Bar (Dublin)

. . . makes Paper stucco in imitation of plaister stucco, not to be distinguished by the best judges, being as sharp, beautiful, and as much relieved as the plaister, etc.

Patrick Gordon acquired patent rights for paperstaining in Ireland in 1692.
[See also 1767.]

1758 R. DOSSIE, *Handmaid to the Arts*, 2 Vols., Octavo (London). (References to Manufacture of Paperhangings, Vol. 2, p. 410, Papier Maché, Marbling, etc.) This work was used very largely by encyclopaedists when writing on these subjects during the eighteenth century, and is unusually precise and detailed in its description of manufacturing processes. [Second Impression, 1764].

Of the vehicles for the colours used either for painting, or forming grounds, for paperhangings. The vehicles for the colours, as before observed, are such as are either formed of water or varnish. When water is used it must be inspissated with size and gum arabic or senegal. The proportion of the size must be adequate to the occasion: for if the different parcels of the size differ greatly in strength no positive rule can be laid down. When the mixture is made for grounds the water should be made as strong of the size as will admit its being commixt with the whiting; and to save expence the gum arabic is sparingly used, or almost wholly omitted in this case. . . .

When varnish is used it must be formed of oil of turpentine and the resins and gums which will dissolve in that menstruum. For common purposes the following composition may be employed: Take of white resin half a pound, of sanderac and mastic, each four ounces, of turpentine two ounces. Powder them and then add two pounds of oil of turpentine: and place the bottle in which the mixture is put in a warm place, where it must remain till the resins etc. be perfectly dissolved. The varnish may be rendered thinner where necessary by increasing the proportion of the oil of turpentine.

1759 THOMAS GRAY writing to Dr. Thomas Warburton (September 18).

I allow tapestry (if at all tolerable) to be a very proper furniture for your sort of house; but doubt if any bargain of that kind is to be met with except at some old mansion sale in the country where People will disdain tapestry because they hear that Paper is all the fashion.

[See also 1760.]

1759 SYMMER, in *Phil. Trans.*, 51, 365.

I was surprised to find it . . . sticking against the paperhangings in my room.

1759 Miller, Architect, whilst working at Hagley. '*Hollier and Bromfield (Bromwich) have writt that the rooms he is to hang will not be fitt to receive the Paper this year.*' *An Eighteenth-century Correspondence*, edited by LILIAN DICKINS and MARY STANTON (1910).

1760 THOMAS GRAY to Mason (June 7):

First and foremost pray take notice of the paper on which I am writing to you; it is the first that ever was made of silk rags . . . it may be of great use for hanging rooms.

1760 'Johann Hautzsch started the first factory to produce regular wallpapers (in Nuremburg).' *Wall Paper Magazine* (U.S.A., 1952).

1760 Madame de Genlis, speaking about fashions in France, '. . . *the ladies wear only robes à l'Anglaise. They even relegate to storage their magnificent Gobelin Tapestries to put English blue paper in their place.*' NANCY MCCLELLAND, *Historic Wallpapers*.
[See 1924.]

At the Blew Paper Warehouse in Aldermanbury LONDON.

Are sold the true sorts of Figured Paper Hangings in pieces of twelve yards long and others after the mode of real Tapistry, and in imitation of Irish Stich, and flowered Damask and also of marble & other Coloured Wainscot, fitt for the hanging of rooms, and stair-Cases, with great variety of Skreens, Chimney pieces, sashes for windows and other things of Curious figures and Colours.

The Patentees for the Sole making thereof doe hereby Signify that their sd pieces are not only more substantial and ornamental as well as Cheaper than the Counterfeits sold in other places but are also distinguished by these words on the back of each piece as their true mark viz.

(Blew Paper Society's Manufacture)

Where are also sold Blew sugar loafe and Purple paper in Reams (they being the only Patentees for the making thereof) and Linnen Cloth Tapistry Hangings very Cheap.

You may observe the following method in the putting up the said figured Paper Hangings.

First Cutt your Breadths to your intended heights then tack them at the top and bottom with Small Tacks, and between each Breadth leave a vacancy of about an inch for the borders to Cover, then cut out the borders into the same lengths and tack them strait down over the Edges of the Breadths and likewise at the top of the room in imitation of a Cornish and the same (if you please) at the bottom as you see described in the figure below without borders and with borders.

But if you will putt up the same without borders, then cutt one of the Edges of each piece or breadth smooth and even, then tack itt about an Inch over the next breadth and so from one to another.

But whether you putt them up with or without Borders gently wett them on the back side with a moist spunge or Cloth which will make them hang the smoother.

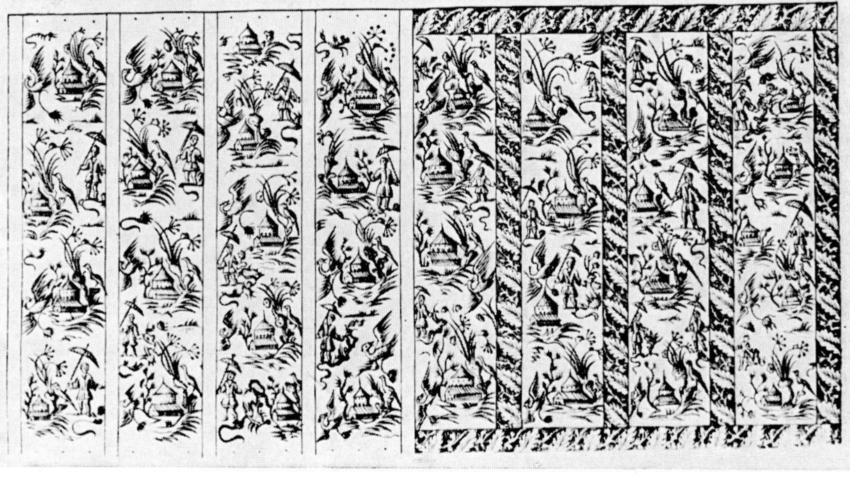

19 Blew Paper Warehouse, Aldermanbury. Advertisement *c.*1700 containing instructions for hanging wallpaper. (Bagford Collection, British Museum)

20 Advertisement, *c*.1720, showing the shop front of The Blew or Blue Paper Warehouse, Aldermanbury, London. Early printing technique is shown in top left-hand panel. (Gough Collection, Bodleian Library, Oxford)

21 Domino paper. Printed in white on a blue ground. In the left-hand lower corner is the signature "Boullard-Neve" (1736–1770). 16½″ × 12½″. French, 18th century. Nancy McClelland, Inc., New York.

Thos Bromwich
At the Golden Lyon on
LUDGATE HILL,
London.
Makes and Sells, all manner of Screens,
Window-Blinds, and Covers for Tables,
Rooms, Cabins, Stair-Cases, &c. Hung
with Guilt Leather, or India Pictures,
Chints's, Callicoes, Cottons, Needlework,
& Damasks Matched in Paper; to the
utmost exactness, at Reasonable Rates.

22 Trade Card of Thomas Bromwich, famous 18th century wallpaper maker, Ludgate Hill, *c.*1740

1761 *Parents' and Guardians' Directory and Youths' Guide in the Choice of a Profession*, by JOSEPH COLLYER (London). '*Of the Paper Hangings Maker. This being a very extensive business that has lately been much improved, etc.*' (Interesting to note that this description was copied word for word by THOMAS MORTIMER in his *Dictionary* of 1766.)

1761 Worshipful Company of Painter-Stainers (London). Thomas Bromwich appointed Master (28 October): Another wallpaper maker was appointed to this high office in 1763. Other Masters in later years were:—Frederick Crace 1851; J. G. Crace 1879; J. D. Crace 1884; Mawer Cowtan 1900; A. B. Cowtan 1922; N. Shand Kydd (wallpaper manufacturer) 1957.

1762 COUNT FREDERICH VON KIELMANSEGG. *Diary of a Journey to England* 1761–2, p. 250. Translated by Countess Kielmansegg, Longmans Green & Co. London, 1902. '*To the ceilings of the rooms, which are prepared, and which have been evenly painted, decorations of papier maché have been added which look like stucco. This material is said to be in general use in London, and I must confess I should never have taken it for what it really is.*' (A reference to a visit to Mrs. Stanley's house in London. Mrs. Stanley was the daughter of Sir Hans Sloane.)

1763 THOMAS MORTIMER. *The Universal Director*. (There is a copy of this rare book in the Guildhall Library.) T.M. gives the names of ten prominent London paperhanging makers. Extract under heading 'Paperhanging Manufacturers':

> *. . . for we annually export vast quantities of this admired article; and the home consumption is not less considerable, as it is not only a cheap, but an elegant part of furniture and saves the builders the expence of wainscotting . . .*'

[See also 1810.]

1764 *The Annual Register* (March 30).

> *The Society of Arts in the Strand have given a premium of £50 to Mr. Benjamin Moore (paperstainer), for the introduction of the manufactory of embossed paper into this kingdom, and making that paper superior to that imported from abroad.*

1764 *The Spirit of the General Letters and Orders of the Board of Excise (for the Guidance of Officers of every Station)*, 1829, p. 236, etc. Reference to year 1764 (July 17): '*Supervisors and Officers must use every likely and legal means to discover where rooms have been hung with plain Paper, and afterwards Stained or Painted.*' [See 1712 Duties, *et seq.*] Typical of many instructions relating to the collection of this revenue, which were issued during the eighteenth century.

1764 M. EDWARD INGRAM. *Leaves from a Family Tree*. [See 1952]. Reference to the decoration of a room in Nathaniel Maister's house at Kilnwick, Yorks. Maister to a Mr. Grimston:

> *I am told there is a new sort of Paper now made for hanging rooms with, which is very handsome, indeed from the price it ought to be so, for I think it is 2/6 a yard. Have you seen any of it? If you have, be so good as to give me your opinion of it.*

[See also 1772].

1765 *Encyclopédie ou Dictionnaire Raisonné, etc.*

DOMINO: a paper on which the tracing, designs or figures, are first printed with clumsily made wooden blocks. The colours are put on afterwards by means of a patron or stencil, as in the case of making playing cards. Domino papers are made particularly in Rouen . . . They are used only by peasants who use them to decorate the upper part of their fireplaces.

DOMINOTIER: One who makes Dominos, marble papers, and self-toned grounded papers. [See 1751].

1766 *Passages from the Diaries of Mrs. Philip Lybbe Powys of Hardwick House, Oxon,* edited by EMILY J. CLIMENSON. Longmans, 1899. August 16. A visit to Lady Orkney's, Taplow '. . . *a Gothic Root house which hangs over the river is exceedingly pretty: the inside is Gothic paper resembling stucco.*' Ensuing entries: September 22, October, 1771, visits to Mawley, and to Fawley Court, Bucks: '*on the left hand of the saloon (at Fawley), is a large billiard room hung with the most beautiful pink India paper, adorn'd with very good prints, the borders cut out and the ornaments put on with great taste by Bromwich*'.

[See also further comments under 1803.]

1766 *Mortimer's New and Complete Dictionary of Trade and Commerce* (London). Brief references under 'Paperhanging's Maker'.

1766 JOHN GWYNN. *London and Westminster Improved—Observation on the State of the Arts* (London).

. . . *Nor is the decoration of the interior parts of buildings better considered: the historical painter is still less attended to than either of these (sculptors, painters, etc.), the grandeur of whose designs is certainly adapted to works of that kind. Instead of being required to give his assistance his part is usually supplied by a paperhanging maker and two or three workers in stucco.*

[See 1756. Isaac Ware.]

1766 JEAN BAPTISTE MICHEL PAPILLON, *Traité Historique et Pratique de la Gravure en Bois,* 2 Vols., 8°, (Paris), begun in 1734. Reference author's description of wallpaper manufacturing processes employed by his father. A very useful source book. C. C. OMAN in *Catalogue of Wallpapers,* 1929, writes: '*Papillon with all his limitations is the primary authority for the history of paperhangings up to the middle of the eighteenth century.*'

1766 *Letters and Journals of Lady Mary Coke,* edited by HON. J. A. HOME (4 vols).

At His Majesty's Lodge in Richmond Park an Indian Paper in the Great Room which cost three guineas the sheet and looks like Japan but the dark blue ground makes the room appear dismal.

[See further references below.]

1766 Inventory of *Sheffield Park, Sussex* (May, 1766). As evidence of the wide use of wallpaper at this date the above inventory mentions the wallpaper in the following rooms: the Green Mowhair room, the Blue Camblet chamber, Lady Cecelia's chamber, Housekeeper's chamber, Lady Diana's chamber, the Sprigg Paper'd chamber, Blue Tent bed chamber, Crimson Morine chamber, etc. [See 'A Sussex Mansion in the Eighteenth Century', by FRANCIS W. STEER, F.S.A. A paper read to the Sussex Arch. Socy., 1956.]

23 J.-B. Michel Papillon (1698–1776), Wood Engraver, Paperstainer and the first historian of wallpaper. Frontispiece to his *Traité Historique*. (*See* 1766)

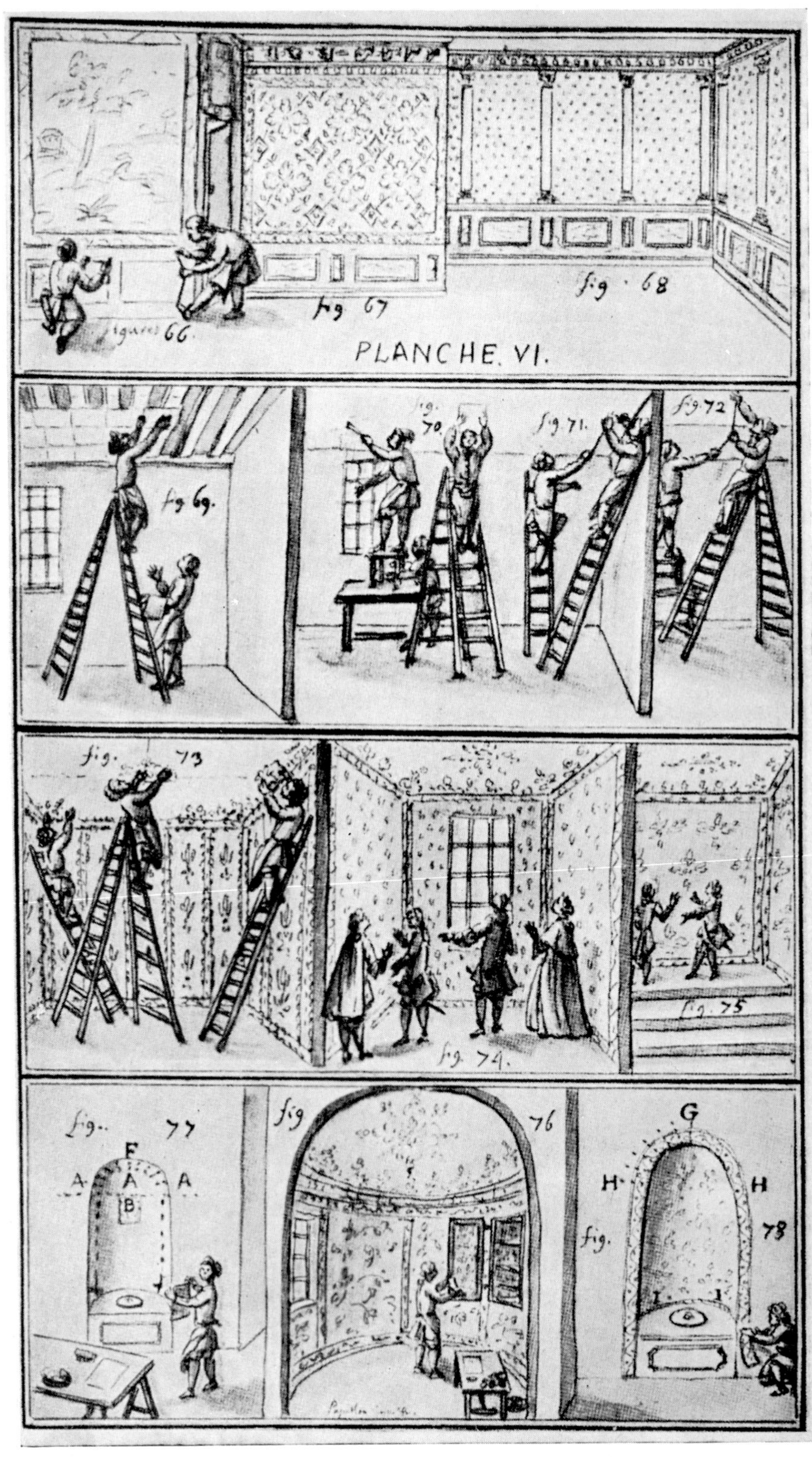

24 Pictorial instructions for hanging wallpaper from *Diderot and d'Alembert's Encyclopaedia*. (*See* 1751)

AN

E S S A Y

ON THE

Invention of Engraving and Printing

IN

CHIARO OSCURO,

AS PRACTISED

By ALBERT DURER, HUGO DI CARPI, &c.

AND

The Application of it to the Making PAPER HANGINGS of Taſte, Duration, and Elegance,

By Mr. JACKSON, of *Batterſea*.

Illuſtrated with PRINTS in proper Colours.

Ceux qui ſont capable d' inventer ſont rares: ceux qui n'inventent point ſont en plus grand nombre, et par conſequent les plus forts.

PASCAL.

LONDON:

Printed for A. MILLAR, in the *Strand*; S. BAKER, in *York-Street, Covent-Garden*; J. WHISTON and B. WHITE; and L. DAVIS, in *Fleet-Street*. MDCCLIV.

(Price Two Shillings and Six-pence.)

25 Title page of John Baptist Jackson's *Essay on Printing in Chiaro Oscuro*, 1754

26 Fragment of 18th century wallpaper pasted on to beams and discovered in 1951 during restoration work at The Feathers' Hotel, Ledbury, Herefordshire

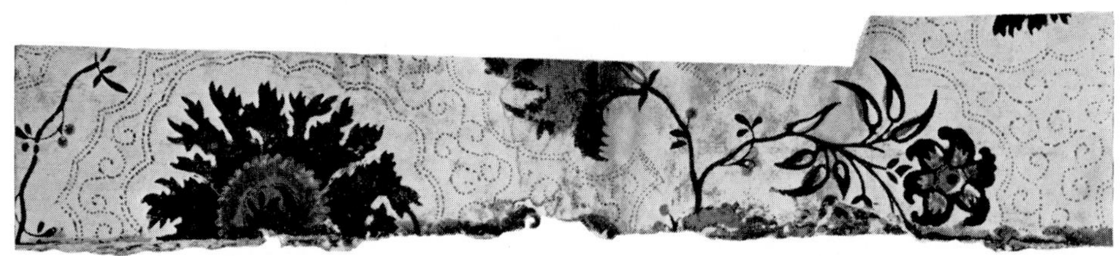

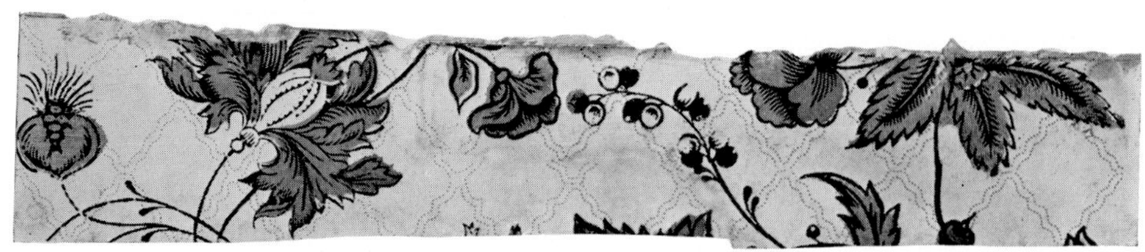

27, 28 Fragments of 18th century wallpaper found at St. Edmund Hall, Oxford

Of the manufacture of paper hangings.

THE paper manufactured for hangings is of ſeveral kinds, ſome being made in repreſentation of ſtucco work, for the covering cielings, or the ſides of halls, ſtair-caſes, paſſages, &c. and others in imitation of velvet, damaſk, brocades, chintz, and other ſuch ſilks and ſtuffs as are employed for hanging rooms. The principal difference in the manufacture lies, however, in the grounds; ſome of which are laid in varniſh, and others in the common vehicles for water colours, and in the raiſing a kind of coloured emboſſment by chopt cloth.

This emboſſed ſort is called *flock-paper*; the art of making which is of very late invention, and is a great improvement of the manufacture of paper hangings, both with regard to the beauty and durableneſs.

Of the unwrought paper proper for hangings.

The kind of paper employed for making the paper hangings is a ſort of coarſe cartoon manufactured for this purpoſe, and there being a particular duty on paper hangings, it is required, under conſiderable penalties, to be ſtamped before it be painted, or otherwiſe decorated for this purpoſe. There is no occaſion however to be more particular in explaining the qualities of this kind of unwrought paper

per

29 Beginning of the chapter on Paperhangings, from Dossie's *Handmaid to the Arts*. (*See* 1758, Robert Dossie)

30 Arabesque design of foliage and flowers in the manner of Jean Pillement's Indian designs. Cream ground, leaves and flowers printed in oranges and blue-greens. French, 1760–65, $40\frac{1}{2}'' \times 26\frac{1}{4}''$. (The Cooper Union Museum, New York)

31 18th century hand-printed wallpaper from an old house in Canterbury

32 Wallpaper book cover printed in distemper by wood blocks, *c.*1760

33 English wallpaper of the late 18th century drawn in ink and water colour and commonly attributed to the Eckhardt Brothers who were famed for their exquisite workmanship in London at this period. This example, from the Victoria and Albert Museum collection, bears the 'G.R.' (Serial letter L) excise stamp on the back.

1767 Advertisement: 'Gordon's Manufactory Warehouse' sells: '*Variety of Papier Maché Ornaments, the best in the Kingdom*'.

1767 Chippendale's men hung the alcove bedchamber at Mersham le Hatch, Kent, with '*12 pieces strip'd verditure set off with* 6 *doz. borders*', *Dict. of English Furniture*, MCQUOID and EDWARDS, 1924.

1768 LADY SHELBORNE'S DIARY (August 20). Reference to Lansdowne House:

> *The attics are all complete, the middle floor we have the Library and three other rooms, all to the Square, which Royle is now busy papering.*

1768 *Journal of Robert Mylne, Architect & Engineer* (1733–1811), by A. E. RICHARDSON, (Batsford, 1955). 8°. February 29 reference, King's Weston, Gloucestershire: '*With Mr. Southwell to Mr. Broomwich* (Bromwich), *for papier maché.*'

1769 *Arthur Young's Travels*. Reference to his visit to Wanstead:

> *We entered the breakfast room elegant indeed, prints pasted on a buff paper, with engraved borders, all disposed in a manner which displays great taste.*

1769 LADY MARY COKE. (January 23.) '*Paid Mr. Bromwich a bill, etc., and gave him further orders.*'

1771 *Journal of The Rt. Hon. Sir Joseph Banks*, 1768–71.

> *A man need go no further to study the Chinese than the Chinese paper. Some of the plants which are common to China and Java as bamboo, are better figured there than in the best botanical authors that I have seen.*

1772 M. GROSLEY, *A Tour to London, or New Observations in England.*

> *. . . with regard to the Walls they are hung with cloth or printed paper by those who are not satisfied with plain wainscot.*

1772 THOMAS MORTIMER, *The Elements of Commerce, Politics and Finances*, London, 4°. The author states:

> *. . . the paperhanging (industry) has lately been introduced into France, with all the necessary tools and implements, straight from the River Thames.*

1772 M. EDWARD INGRAM, *Leaves from a Family Tree* (1952). This book contains many references to eighteenth-century wallpapers including the following. [See also under 1952.] Reference to the decoration of Kilnwick, Yorks.

> *Our people, (Elwick, Upholsterer), set off yesterday to York. There will be business sufficient for them to go on with while you will be engaged, in putting up the plane paper in the Drawing Room, Library and Yellow bedchamber preparing Colour etc. . . . that is they was to put on the paper, as that is always put up and colour'd after.*

1772 SCHAEFFER, J. C. '*Erweis in Musterbogen das die neuen Papierarten sich allerdings auch zu Tapeten übermahlen und gebrauchen lassen.*' 12 specimens. Mentioned in B.M. Subject Index and also Peddie.

1772 PETER QUENNELL, *Four Portraits. Studies of the Eighteenth Century* (Collins, London, 1945). Reference to Edward Gibbon's house, No. 7 Bentinck Street:

> *which he proceeded to equip in the height of contemporary taste. Thus, for the library, naturally the most important room, he selected "a fine shag flock paper"* . . .

1772 LADY MARY COKE'S *Journal*. '*I called on the Duchess of Norfolk and found her sorting butterflies cut out of India paper for a room she is going to furnish.*' (E. JORDAN in the *Decorator* 23 - 8 - 09, p. 55, states that this practice was referred to as 'paper mosaic' work.)

1773 (August 1.) Paper printed, painted or stained was permitted to be imported after this date on paying, in addition to the customs already imposed, a duty of $1\frac{1}{2}$*d.* per square yard. Paper of the manufacture of 'India', imported by the East India Company, was exempted from the duty. (13 Geo. III, c. 67). *Macpherson's Annals of Commerce*, 1805.

1773-4 Mrs. Delany commenced her folio volumes of paper flowers (now in the B.M. Print Room). Writing in *Country Life* (January 25, 1952) BERNARD and THERLE HUGHES state:

> *The sheet of thick paper forming the background to each flower is painted a full opaque black, being prepared by a paper-stainer. From the same source she obtained many of the coloured papers with which she created the flowers* . . .

1774 Anthony George Eckhardt of Chelsea (paperhanging maker), elected Fellow of the Royal Society.
[See 1786, Whiteland's Works, etc.]

1774 *Practical Magazine* (U.S.A.) contains reference to the Manufacture of Paperhangings.

1774 Manuscripts of Lord Kenyon. Hist: MSS: Commission 14th Report. Letter from Mrs. Kenyon describing new house at 18 Lincoln's Inn Fields, London.

> *The entrance is a broad lobby well lighted by a window over the door . . . it is wainscot painted white. The dining room is 21′ × 17′ wide and is to be new papered this week. The paper is to be a blue small patterned flock. I will send you a bit of it. Our lodging room is hung with a green flock paper.*

1774 Letters and Journals of LADY MARY COKE (1756–74). '*Notting Hill, Friday ye 2nd Sept. 1774.*' Reference Lady Bute's: '*Almost all the rooms are hung with light green plain papers which show the pictures to great advantage.*'

1775 JAMES BOSWELL, *Life of Johnson* (October 14).

> *We went to the house of Mr. Argenson, . . . the ladies' closet wainscotted with large squares of glass over painted paper . . .*

[See also 1778 below.]

1775 MRS. THRALE'S *French Journal* (November 4), at Cambrai:

> *Here are paperhangings too, to my chamber, and a Blue and White check bed and it all looks much nearer home than France does.*

34 Wallpaper printed from wood blocks in distemper colours. English, 1765. (Cooper Union Museum, New York)

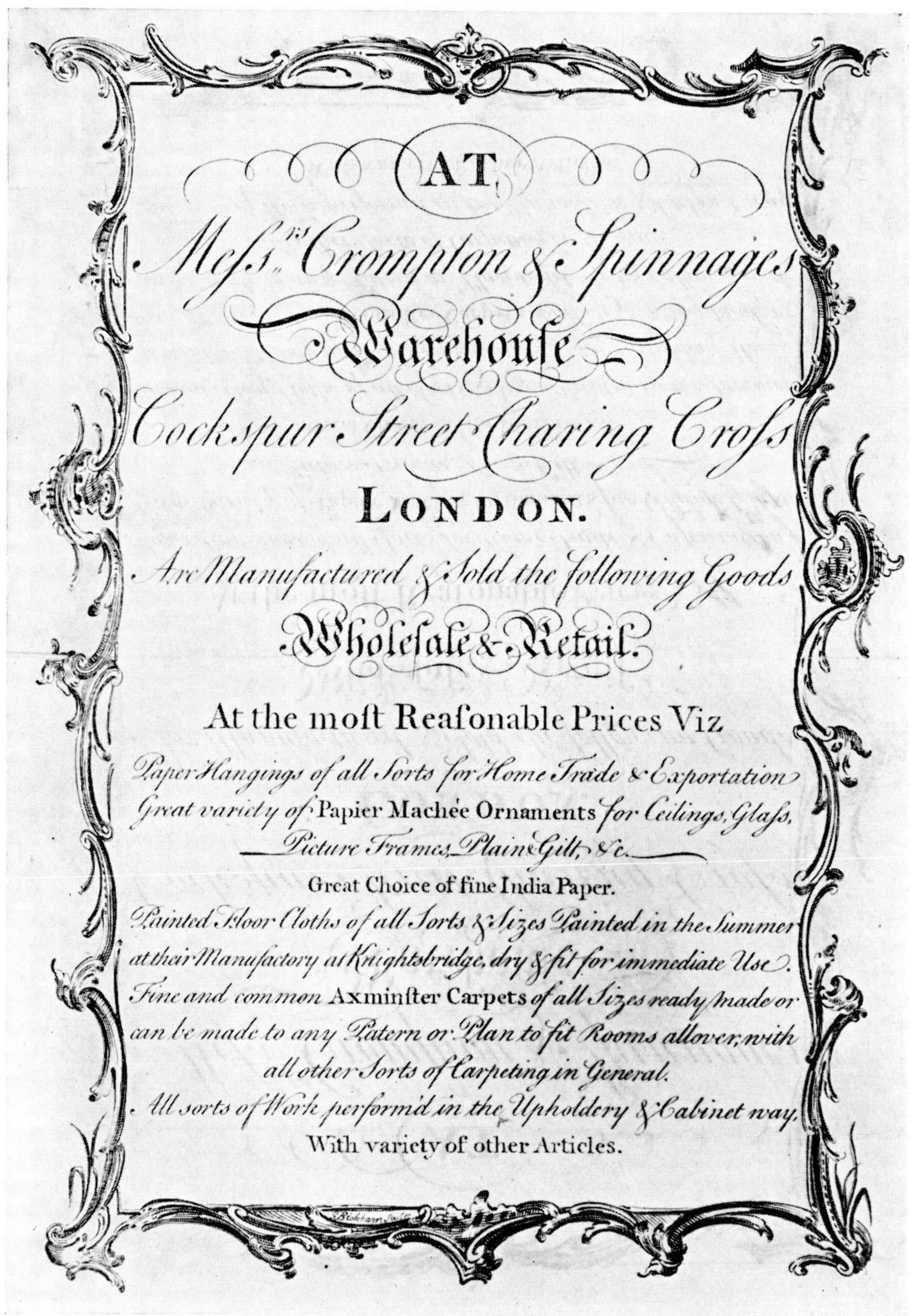

AT
Mess.rs Crompton & Spinnages
Warehouse
Cockspur Street Charing Cross
LONDON.
Are Manufactured & Sold the following Goods
Wholesale & Retail.
At the most Reasonable Prices Viz
Paper Hangings of all Sorts for Home Trade & Exportation
Great variety of Papier Machée Ornaments for Ceilings, Glass,
Picture Frames, Plain & Gilt, &c.
Great Choice of fine India Paper.
Painted Floor Cloths of all Sorts & Sizes Painted in the Summer
at their Manufactory at Knightsbridge, dry & fit for immediate Use.
Fine and common Axminster Carpets of all Sizes ready made or
can be made to any Patern or Plan to fit Rooms allover, with
all other Sorts of Carpeting in General.
All sorts of Work perform'd in the Upholdery & Cabinet way.
With variety of other Articles.

35 Crompton & Spinnage. Trade card issued by this wallpaper firm towards the end of the 18th century

1777 MARY HAMILTON'S *Diary* (August). Queen Charlotte employed wallpaper when fitting up Queen's Lodge, Windsor at this date.

1778 *Instructions for Collectors, Supervisors and Officers in the Country* (London). Reference to collection of wallpaper duties, etc. Very useful book to be seen in the Library of H.M. Customs & Excise.

[See also 1781, 1792, etc.]

1778 Petition addressed to Lord North by London paperstainers begging him to extend wallpaper tax to wall paintings.

1778 HORACE WALPOLE to Earl Harcourt (October).

I have kept your servant while I hunted for the 'treillage' paper, but I cannot find it. The roses were not interlaced among the batons but seemed tacked against them which, had I had it executed here I intended should be corrected.

1778 JAMES BOSWELL, *Life of Johnson.* Reference to Mrs. Thrale's Print Room at Streatham, where, '*amongst the prints pasted on the walls*' were those from HOGARTH'S *Modern Midnight Conversations.*

1779 Newspaper advertisement. Source unknown.

NEW invented PAPER HANGINGS by DARLY and EDWARDS, Painters and Engravers, at the Golden Acorn facing Hungerford Market, superior and cheaper than anything of the kind. Gentry waited on with Designs in any Taste. Rooms neatly fitted up on an entire new Plan; and old Papers mended.*

* Matthias Darly engraved many plates in CHIPPENDALE'S *Gentleman's and Cabinet Makers' Directory.*

1780 JOHANN WOLFGANG VON GOETHE, *Dichtung und Warheit—Aus meinem Leben,* 1811. Reference his friend Nothnagel who made wallcoverings in Frankfurt. The poet writes:

In a very large room every kind of wall covering was being processed, from the raw material to the finished product, on which the most wonderful designs were printed . . . chinoiseries, and fantastic motifs, life-like flowers and figures as well as landscapes laid on with the painter's skilled brush. I was delighted with their endless variety.

[A number of Goethe's references to wallpaper appear in De Francesco's article, CIBA Review 1937].

1781 *Instructions for the Officers who survey Paper-Stainers in London* (to be seen in H.M. Customs & Excise Library).

You are to survey your traders (if consistent with your other necessary business), every day or otherwise, as your Surveyor shall think needful . . . and on each survey you are to examine the paper in operation carefully, in order to see that the same is Stamped that the Revenue be not defrauded by the traders printing paper not being stamped.

1781 The Hon. John Byng, later 5th Viscount Torrington. Reference visit to Hagley House,

. . . the house is ill situated . . . the inside is tawdrily and badly fitted up with carving, gilding, Chinese paper, etc.

INSTRUCTIONS

FOR

OFFICERS

WHO SURVEY

Paper-Makers, and Paper-Stainers

IN THE

COUNTRY.

LONDON:

PRINTED IN THE YEAR M,DCC,LXXXI.

36 For Extract from this publication see 1781

1781 William Beckford. *Works of Bentham*, ed. JOHN BOWRING, p. 285, Vol. X, 1843.

When about to sleep at an inn he (Beckford) orders it to be papered for him at the expense of £10, like Wolsey who travelled with a set of gold hangings.

1783

Réveillon (French wallpaper maker) and Etienne Montgolfier (Architect and Balloonist) (September 12). [See Musée Galliéra, Paris, 1933.]

Montgolfier's balloon, a fire balloon, rose some distance in the air from the grounds of Réveillon's wallpaper factory (Faubourg St. Antoine, Paris) before being completely destroyed by a storm. [See also Thomas Carlyle, 1789.]

37 Montgolfier's Fire Balloon—from the Catalogue of the Musée Galliéra Exhibition

1786 Whiteland's Works, Chelsea. '*a large and spacious mansion . . . was for some time in the possession of Messrs. Eckhardts (paperstainers), who first established it in partnership with Mr. Woodmason in 1786*, from *FAULKNER's* Chelsea. 1829.

1786 SOPHIE VON LA ROCHE, *Sophie in London* (Cape, London, 1933). Reference to her visit to London at this date and to Seddon's Furniture Works:

He employs 400 on any work connected with the making of household furniture; joiners, carvers, gilders, mirror workers, upholsterers She also saw *chintz, wool and silk materials for curtains and bed covers, hangings in every possible material.*

1786 Advertisement in American newspaper:

Flies and smoke operate to soil paper in common rooms if the goods are too delicate; to prevent which I have pin-grounds that fly marks will not be perceptible upon. Also dark grounds which the smoke will not considerably affect in the course of twenty years, at such low prices will eventually be found cheaper than whitewash.

1787 *Gentleman's Magazine* (July). Obituary, Thomas Bromwich:

who had acquired a genteel fortune, on Ludgate Hill, by his ingenuity in manufacturing paperhangings in imitation of stucco work, as well as of damasks, brocades, and other stuffs employed for hanging rooms.

1788 *Hamwood Papers of the Ladies of Llangollen*, etc., edited by MRS. G. H. BELL, 1930. Writing under date July 13, 1788.

Arrived at Oswestry at half past 6. Found the Barretts in the bedroom . . . the drawing room still unfinished. They showed us various patterns they had received from London, of Woodmason's new invented paper. Never more disappointed. Dingy. Wholly deficient in colour, lustre, and effect.

1788 BRISSOT DE WARVILLE, *Nouveau Voyage dans les États Unis de l'Amérique*, 3 Vols., (Paris). Report on visit to New York.

The happy invention of coloured paper for hanging . . . will subsist for a long time because it gives a neat and agreeable appearance to dwellings.

1788 EPHRAIM CHAMBERS, F.R.S. *Cyclopaedia*, or *An Universal Dictionary of Arts and Sciences.* (London). This edition contains useful entry under 'Paperhangings' relating to Manufacturing, which might be based on DOSSIE'S *Handmaid to the Arts.* First Edition of this Encyclopaedia, 1728.

1788-97 *Encyclopaedia Britannica* (3rd Edn.):

Method of painting the paper hangings. There are three methods by which paper-hangings are painted; the first by printing *on the colours; the second by using the* stencil; *and the third by laying them on with a* pencil, *as in other kinds of painting.*

When colours are laid on by printing, the impression is made by wooden prints; which are cut in such manner, that the figure to be expressed is made to project from the surface by cutting away all the other part; and this, being charged with the colours tempered with their proper vehicle, by letting it gently down on a block on which the colour is previously spread, conveys it from thence to the ground of the paper, on which it is made to fall more forcibly by means of its weight, and the effort of the arm of the person who uses the print. It is easy to conclude, that there must be as many separate prints as there are colours to be printed. But where there are more than one, great care must be taken, after the first, to let the print fall exactly in the same part of the paper as that which went before; otherwise the figure of the design would be brought into irregularity and confusion. In common paper of low price, it is usual, therefore, to print only the outlines, and lay on the rest of the colours by stencilling; which both saves the expense of cutting more prints, and can be practised by common workmen, not requiring the great care and dexterity necessary to the using of several prints.

1789 Illustrations of Contemporary Wallpapers. [See engravings of George Morland's pictures 'Industry' and 'Dressing for the Masquerade' Lætitia Series, 1789.]

1789 THOMAS CARLYLE, *The French Revolution.* Describing a riot which broke out at Réveillon's wallpaper factory in the Rue St. Antoine, Paris:

The Sieur Réveillon, extensive Paper Manufacturer of the Rue St. Antoine, he commonly so punctual, is absent from the Electoral Committee and even will never reappear there. In those 'immense magazines of velvet paper' has aught befallen? Alas, yes . . . Was the Sieur Réveillon, himself once a journeyman, heard to say that a journeyman might live handsomely on fifteen sous a day? Some sevenpence halfpenny . . . or was he only thought, and believed, to be heard saying it?

[See also *A. H. Dampmartin* (Berlin, 1799), i, 25–7, for a description of this riot which may have sparked off the French Revolution.]

38 Wallpaper printed from wood blocks. Part of an unused length in the possession of the Cooper Union Museum, New York. English, 1765

Sr. London June 26th 1783

P Wm Cave ye York Carrier
yesterday morning I sent ye India paper
hangings which I hope will come safe
& meet with approbation, I have put a Chineese
ornament round ye Top, by order ye Bishop of [illegible]
which I hope will also please I have markt out
peice with a number & Enclosd ye plann
of ye room to answer ye same, I have not recd
ye Box of paper as yet but so soon as ever it comes I will
very Willingly send you anything you shall please
to Order from Sr

Your Most Obedient
Humble Servt

Thos Bromwich

ye Carrier promises
to diliver ye Case ye 2d of July.

39 Letter from Thomas Bromwich of Ludgate Hill, London, dated June 26, 1783

1790 *London Gazette* April 3–6. Partnership between Messrs. Bowers, Eckhardt & Co. of Old Bond St., *Paperhangings manufacturers, is dissolved by mutual consent. Business to be carried on at the same place by Messrs. Bowers & Co. London Gazette* (*June 12–15*). Partnership between Thomas Martyn and John Sherringham, *Decorators in Ornamental Paperhangings, Great Marlborough St., dissolved this day* (*June 15*), *by mutual consent. Debts, etc., to Mr. William Clark, 38 New Bond St.*

1792 *Index to the Laws of Excise from 1 Jac., 1 to 32 Geo., 3.* [See Paper for Hangings]. This register contains over sixty references to the Acts, or Chapters of Acts, relating to the operation of the Wallpaper Tax. (To be seen in the Library of H.M. Customs & Excise.)

1792 IRIS BROOKE, *Four Walls Adorned* [Methuen 1952.] p. 115.

> *This year Lord Macartney of Coutts Bank and a few of his especial friends had hand-painted Chinese wallpapers sent from China to decorate their homes. The example now at Coutts Bank is famous and has been admired and discussed for 150 years, but there are still a number of others similar in design to be 'discovered' in other houses in England. At Ramsbury near Marlborough there is a little study with a full scenic wallpaper in nearly perfect condition . . . This paper came to England on the same ship as that of Lord Macartney's and was probably 'hung' within the year.*

[See also 1820.]

1793 THOMAS SHERATON, *Cabinet Makers' and Upholsterers' Drawing Book* (London). Vol. II., '. . . *A drawing room is of that sort which admits of the highest taste and elegance*'. The author goes on to specify wallpaper for the panelled walls, examples of which are illustrated. The Eckhardts of Chelsea were subscribers to this book.

1793 F. Eckhardt patented a process for making gold and silver paperhangings. Patent No. 1953:

> *Invention and Method of Preparing and Printing Paper in different Patterns, and to silver it over with Fine Silver Leaves, so as to resemble Damask Lace and various Silk Stuffs to be used for Hangings and other Furniture for Rooms.*

1795 R. ACKERMANN. *Repository of Arts and Manufactures* (London), reprinted 1809–29, 4th Edn. Fugitive references to wallpaper. [See 1819].

1795 *New Royal Encyclopaedia*, GEORGE SELBY HOWARD, F.R.S. Contains a full entry under 'Paperhangings', Vol. III, p. 1556, but quite obviously inspired by other encyclopaedias, notably *Encyclopaedia Britannica*, 1788, etc. ' . . . *furniture now greatly used and approved as it is at once airy and cheap.*'

1796 *Journal für Fabrik Manufactur, Handlung und Mode* (*échantillons de papiers français*). (Leipzig), January–June, p. 237.

1796 J. G. Hancock patented a device for making embossed paperhangings.

1797 PROFESSOR JOHANN BECKMANN, *History of Inventions*, 1st edition. 1797; 2nd edition, 1814; 3rd edition, 1817; 4th edition, 1846. Contains useful entry under 'Paperhangings'.

Among the most elegant . . . may be reckoned those which imitate so exactly every variety of marble, porphyry, and other species of stones that when the walls of an apartment are neatly covered with them, the best connoisseur may not, without close examination, be able to discover the deception.

1801 PAPERMAKING Louis Robert takes out a Patent in France covering the invention of a machine capable of producing paper in 'endless lengths'. See 1857 *Journal of the R.S.A.* This patent subsequently paved the way for the perfecting of a wallpaper printing machine.

1801 M. KOOPS, '*painted or stained paper is the most beautiful, the cleanest and the cheapest ornament for furnishing rooms*'.

1803 *Diary of* MRS. PHILIP LYBBE POWYS (February 25):

. . . She has an elegant house in the Crescent (Bath), and he has one in St. James' Square, Bath, which though most elegantly furnished, after he returned from Paris finding paperhangings were there call'd vulgar, immediately took all down and hung all with satins.

1805 *Dictionnaire Universel de Commerce, Banque, Manufactures, Douanes, Peche, Navigation Marchande . . .,* F. BUISSON, ed. (Paris), Vol. 2, p. 337.

1805 DAVID MACPHERSON'S *Annals of Commerce.* [See 1773.]

1806 C. A. OGLANDER, *Nunwell Symphony,* (1945). John Nash (Architect). Reference to his work at Nunwell, I.O.W., at this period.

John Nash, who lived at Cowes, . . . persuaded William Oglander that the oak panelling in many of the rooms was sombre and unhygienic and charged him £3000 for tearing it out and replacing it with wallpaper.

1807 *The Ambulator, or a Pocket Companion in a Tour round London, Under* Chelsea.

On the site of a once celebrated manufactory of porcelain (in an old mansion by the waterside) has been a manufactory of stained paper, stamped after a peculiar manner, the invention of Messrs. Eckhardts who likewise established at Whitelands House, in 1791, a new and beautiful manufacture of painted silk, varnished linen, cloths, paper, etc. . . .

1808 CROSBY'S *Merchants' and Tradesman's Pocket Dictionary.*

Paper-Stainer. This, which is a very profitable business, is similar to that of calico printing, and with respect to those who undertake it, nearly similar qualifications are necessary and large premises. A considerable stock in trade is also requisite.

1809 Act: 49 George III, *c.* 81. Licences for paperstaining businesses raised to £20 per annum.

1810 THOMAS MORTIMER, *A General Dictionary of Commerce, Trade and Manufactures* (London). Second Edition, 1819. (There is also a description of the manufacture of Flock papers, etc.) (*continued on page 71*).

40 Typical detail from a late 18th century Chinese painted wallpaper, formerly at Avebury Manor, Wilts.

ROYAL PATENT MANUFACTORY

OF

PAINTED SILK, VARNISHED-LINEN, CLOTH, PAPER, &c. &c.

FOR

HANGINGS, AND OTHER ARTICLES OF FURNITURE,

UNDER THE PATRONAGE OF

HER ROYAL HIGHNESS THE PRINCESS ROYAL,

AT OLD WHITELAND'S HOUSE, KING'S-ROAD, CHELSEA.

MESS. ECKHARDTS and Co. having brought their Manufactory to that Degree of Perfection which they flatter themfelves will meet with the Approbation of the Public, beg leave to explain the feveral Branches wherein they are concerned.

Their Manufactory confifts of every Thing that belongs to the fitting-up of Houfes, moft particularly that Branch that relates to the ornamental part of Dreffing Rooms, Bed Chambers, Halls, Eating and Drawing Rooms.

Thefe, in their feveral Modes, are fo appropriated to the various Defcriptions of Houfes, that the Expence may fuit Perfons in every Clafs of Life.

Papers, on a new Principle, in a diverfity of beautiful Patterns, and of all Prices.

Varnifhed Linen, and Silk Oil Cloth, in a variety of elegant Defigns.

Painted Silks, and Sattins, in the utmoft degree of Style, and richnefs of Compofition; as alfo, Paintings on Cloth, Caffimere, Leather, and other Subftances, fo as to form a moft extenfively varied Collection of Articles, for Hangings and other ornamental Parts of Furniture: all perfectly free from any difagreeable Smell.

Their *Patent Silver Damafk varnifhed Linen*, and *Paper*, they particularly recommend to the attention of the Public, who may reft affured, that, in addition to their acknowledged Elegance, by a Procefs, with great Labour, Perfeverance, and Expence,

41 Advertisement, *c.*1790, issued by the Eckhardt Brothers—famous 18th century wallpaper makers

42 Late 18th century wallpaper in the Round Room, Moccas Court, Herefordshire, *c.*1780. Panels 9 feet 9 inches long. Possibly produced by Eckhardt Brothers, Chelsea

43 Wallpaper printed by Réveillon, Paris, used as a cover for a small book of French poems, *c*.1790 (about actual size)

44 Hand printed English wallpaper, *c.*1790–1800, from George Hill House, Robertsbridge, Sussex. Printed in reds and greens on a light green ground

45 Multi-coloured flock wallpaper entitled 'Les Deux Pigeons.' Produced by Réveillon, Paris. Late 18th century. Now to be seen at Clandon Park, near Guildford, Surrey. (See *Architectural Review* 1951)

46 A trade card designed by Darly, Cranbourn Alley, London, for Davenport's of Pall Mall, *c.*1790

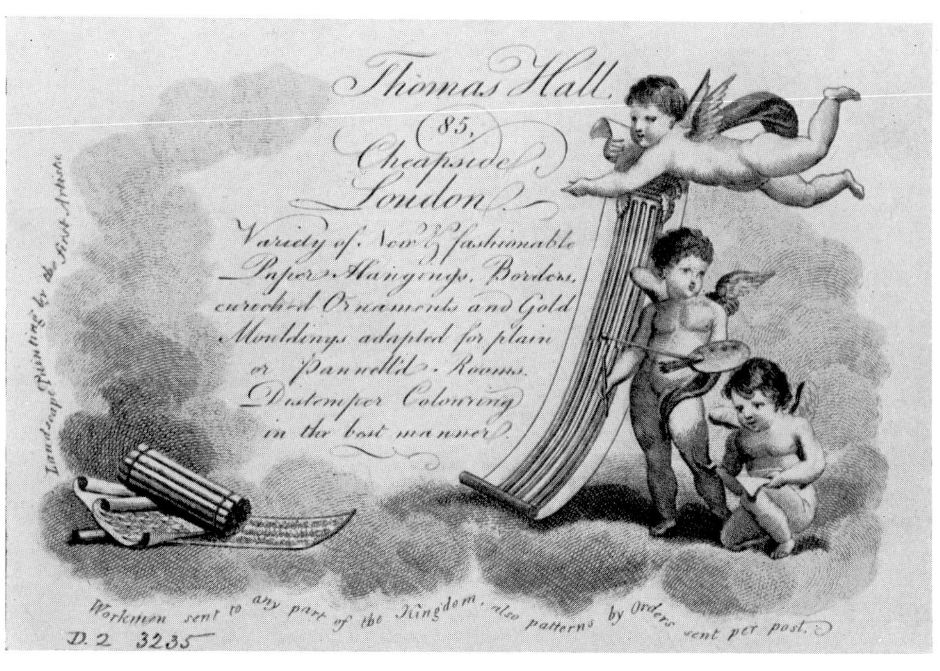

47 Trade card issued by Thomas Hall, 85, Cheapside, London, *c.*1800

48 Late 18th century Chinese wallpaper. (Victoria and Albert Museum)

49 Part of a French panoramic wallpaper, hand printed, probably by J. Zuber et Cie, Rixheim, early 19th century. The German Wallpaper Museum at Kassel has a set of this fine decoration

50 Fragment of late 18th century hand printed wallpaper after a design by Thomas Sheraton. An illustration from MacIver Percival's series of articles in *The Journal of Decorative Art* 1925

Paperhangings are made in several different ways. Some are printed from wooden blocks and coloured by placing paper over them, cut out in spaces in the forms of the figures, or parts of the figures where they are to be laid on . . . other kinds of paperhangings are made without their being first printed (*on*) *blocks, solely by means of papers cut into sprigs and flowers which are laid on as in the other case, and the figures represented on the paper by brushing over these patterns, which are removed as before till all the different colours and shades are given and the work completed.*

1810 From *The Daily Herald*, October 25, 1957. (Apocryphal.) A reply to a correspondent's letter deploring the use of ultra modern colour schemes in wallpapers:

This reminds me of a story of Napoleon's Josephine. She learned that a woman she detested was coming to her reception in a green dress, so she had her drawing room completely re-decorated in a curious shade of blue. This provided a perfect setting for her own dress—and made her rival's green look hideous.

1810–11 LOUIS SIMOND, a French American on a visit to England. ['Journal of a Tour' in Great Britain.]

Inside the principal room furnished with prints pasted on a yellow wall, with a very narrow paper border, and prettily arranged.

1811 THOMAS JEFFERSON HOGG. *Percy Bysshe Shelley*, [See also DOWDEN'S *Life of Shelley*]. Reference to the poet's search for lodgings in London at this date:

. . . the walls had lately been covered with trellised paper; in those days it was not common. There were trellises, vine leaves, with their tendrils and huge clusters of grapes, green and purple. This was delightful, he went close up to the wall and touched it: 'We must stay here; stay for ever.'

1809-12 MARIA EDGWORTH, *Vivian* Chap. XIII. '*The vulgar present full of upholsterers and paperhangers . . . pressed upon his attention with importunate claims.* Also in her novel, *The Absentee* (1812), reference to '*Trebisond Trellice paper*'. (Fully described in METFORD WARNER'S Paper which was read to The Institute of British Decorators in London, in 1910.)

1813 *Autobiography of Leigh Hunt*, Chap. XIV. Reference to his imprisonment at this date:

I papered the walls with a trellis of roses; I had the ceiling coloured with clouds and sky; the barred windows I screened with Venetian blinds . . . Charles Lamb declared there was no other such room, except in a fairy tale.

1813 *Pantologia. A New Cyclopaedia*, JOHN MASON GOOD, F.R.S. See Vol. IX under Paperhangings.

Mr. John Middleton lately communicated some improvements in the printing of paperhangings to the Society of Arts. They are intended to facilitate the conveyance of the paper over the printing table and to give a greater pressure than usual to the block when printing dark grounds.

c. 1813 GUSTAVE FLAUBERT, '*Un coeur simple*'. Short story which appeared in 1877 in *Le Moniteur Universel*, and refers to the early nineteenth century.

. . . Au premier étage il y avait d'abord la chambre de '*Madame*', *très grande, tendue d'un papier à fleurs pâles.*

1813 SACHEVERELL SITWELL *Portugal and Madeira*, (Batsford, 1954), in a description of the Palace of Queluz, mentions the destruction by fire (1934):

> *of a unique pictorial wallpaper, probably of French manufacture, illustrating the Greek War of Independence, in which the figure of Lord Byron could be seen among the white kilted Evzones, but apart from this loss the rooms to-day appear in much the same state as they must have been at the end of the eighteenth century when the palace was completed.*

1813 SIR THOMAS LAWRENCE, P.R.A. Reference to wallpaper in his house at 65 Russell Square. '. . . *Thus I suffered a yellow paper to remain that I knew was hurtful to my pictures. It is now a rich crimson Paper with a border. My little room beyond it is fitted in the same way and is a sweet, precious Room.*'

From *Regency Portrait Painter*, DOUGLAS GOLDRING, (Macdonald, London, 1951).

1816 ELIZABETH YATES, *Patterns on the Wall*, (New York, 1946). The action of this novel hinges on the year 1816. '*I tell you sir,*' *the stranger was saying emphatically*, '*more and more people are coming to realise that walls of wood or plaster won't do. They're to be painted with scenes like those costly French wallpapers that are being imported. . . .*'

1816 Essay by LEIGH HUNT, *The Old Lady*. Reference to the inside of her house being wainscot and not papered.

1818 GEORGE SAND writes of her room in a Paris convent at this period: '*The wallpaper was once yellow, or so I am told. However that may be I find it a source of constant interest for it is scribbled all over with names, mottoes, verses, all sorts of foolishness, reflections and dates, the relics of former occupants . . .*'

ANDRÉ MAUROIS, *Lélia—the Life of George Sand*, 1952–3. (Jonathan Cape, London.)

1819 ABRAHAM REES. *Cyclopaedia, or Universal Dictionary of Arts, Sciences and Literature*, 4 Vols. See under 'Paperhangings'. Useful account of contemporary manufacturing practice.

> *Paperhangings may be spangled with a kind of talc. Smalt may also be used in the same manner as flock or spangles. But hangings of this kind are now little used.*

1819 ACKERMANN'S *Repository of Arts*, Vol. VII, p. 269. Reference to Brunell's Patent Metallick Paper. *Now used by skilful artists with great success in decorating apartments.* [See 1795.]

1819 PYNE'S 'History of the Royal Residences.' Reference to flock wallpaper in the King's (William III) Great Drawing Room.

1819 HONORÉ DE BALZAC in the novel *Old Goriot* writes,

> *. . . the flooring of the room is uneven. Its walls are panelled to elbow level, and above that the rest of the wall is hung with a varnished paper on which the principal scenes from Telemaque are depicted, with the classical characters in colour. The wall space between . . . displays to boarders the feats given to the son of Ulysses by Calypso.* (*continued on page 75*)

51 English chinoiserie panel. Late 18th century. Ink or water colour and etched outline. Size approx. 4 wide × $3\frac{1}{2}'$ high

52 Chinese painted wallpaper in a room at Woburn Abbey. Late 18th century

(The above reference describes one of the French scenic papers, 'Télemaque dans l'Isle de Calypso' printed by Dufour about this date.) and:

Eugénie Grandet (written 1833 but refers to early years of the nineteenth century).

> *Charles stood aghast amid his trunks. His glance took in the sloping walls of an attic room hung with the kind of paper, yellow and strewn with bouquets of flowers, favoured by country inns. . . .'*

1819 *Journal of Gideon Mantell*, Surgeon, of Lewes, Sussex. (Oxford University Press, 1940), under date June 26:

> *Received the Gothic paper for the Staircase from my brother-in-law, James Woodhouse.*

1820 THOMAS CREEVEY, M.P., writing about the decorations in Buckingham Palace at this date:

> *It has cost a million of money and there is not a fault that has not been committed in it . . . Instead of being called Buckingham Palace it should be the Brunswick Hotel. Raspberry coloured pillars without end that quite turn me sick to look at . . . but the Queen's papers, for her own apartments, far exceed everything else in their ugliness and vulgarity.*

(This refers to Queen Adelaide's wallpapers—the date is more likely to be 1834 when the rebuilding and furnishing was completed).

1820 IRIS BROOKE, *Four Walls Adorned*, (Methuen, 1952). Reference to this period:

> *The stage was now set for the entrance of the Interior Decorator, and he made his debut appropriately in an avalanche of fringed draperies, gorgeous lighting effects . . . etc. As this gentleman's livelihood was dependent on his ability to make yesterday's fashion an unforgiveable offence, the mere walls of a room became the background for the paperhangers repertoire and the setting for the rapidly changing scene.* [See above 1792].

1821 *Encyclopaedia Londinensis*, or *Universal Dictionary of Arts, Sciences and Literature*, compiled by JOHN WILKES, of Sussex. Very useful article on 'Paperhanging', see p. 377, Vol. XVIII.

> *There are various kinds of paperhangings of which some are made in the representation of stucco-work for covering ceilings or the sides of halls, staircases, passages, etc., and others in imitation of velvet, damask, brocades, chintzes or such stuffs as are employed for hanging rooms . . For common designs done with water only: the following are most proper:*

For RED:	*Lake, rose pink, vermilion.*
BLUE:	*Prussian blue, verditer, and indigo.*
YELLOW:	*Yellowberry wash, Dutch pink, yellow ochre.*
GREEN:	*Verdigris, or a mixture of blue and yellow.*
ORANGE:	*Vermilion or Red Lead; with Dutch pink.*
PURPLE:	*A wash made of Log wood, or a mixture of the Lake, or rose pink, with deep coloured Prussian blue or with Indigo.*
BLACK:	*Ivory black, and in some nicer cases, lamp-black.*
WHITE:	*Whiting; and for the heightenings, white lead.*

1822 SIR WALTER SCOTT. An anecdote about this great man by his decorator, D. R. Hay. [See 1847.]

Sir Walter told me to cover the remainder of the wall (of the Dining room at Abbotsford), and gave me an 'Indian' paper of a crimson colour, with a small gilded pattern upon it. This paper, he said, he did not altogether approve of for a dining room but as he had got it in a present expressly for that purpose, and as he believed it to be rare, he would have it put upon that room, rather than hurt the feelings of the donor.

1823 J. BADCOCK. *Dom. Amusem.* 170. '*Walls . . . may be papered immediately.*'

1823 *Encyclopaedia Britannica*, 6th Edn. See under 'PAPER':

White and Coloured Grounds for paperhangings. The common grounds laid in water are made by mixing whiting with the common glovers' size, and laying it on the paper with a proper brush in the most even manner. When coloured grounds are required the same method must be pursued and the ground of whiting first laid; except in pale colours, such as straw colours or pink where a second coating may sometimes be spared by mixing some strong colour with the whiting.

1824 *The Original Picture of London.* Re-edited by J. BRITTON, F.S.A.

The Oil Cloth and Paperhanging Manufactories, in various parts of the suburbs, are on a large scale, and challenge curiosity.

[See also George Dodd's 1843 reference below].

1824 Cowtan & Sons Ltd. (formerly Interior Decorators, Oxford St., London). 24 Order Books covering wallpaper sales from 1824 to 1938, containing cuttings of wallpaper and other materials sold by this firm for interior decoration. Presented to the Victoria and Albert Museum by Mr. A. L. Cowtan in memory of his father, Arthur Barnard Cowtan.

1824 Extract from a letter to the customers of MM. Dufour and Leroy, famous wallpaper manufacturers, Paris:

Août 1824 . . . Nous osons nous flatter que rien ne manque à notre assortiment. Satins de divers genres; iris; dessins en velouté imitant les plus belles tentures de soie: petits décors; décors riches; passe partouts; dessus de portes et devans de cheminées en grisaille et en coloris; bordures d'ornemens en détrempe et en velouté corniche, lambris; enfin un paysage en camaïeux de 30 lés, sur grand papier répresentant un sujet aussi intéressant que gracieux, l'histoire de Paul et Virginie.

1825 R. W. SYMONDS, 'From Thomas Chippendale to George Smith', *Connoisseur*, June, 1953.

The first quarter of the nineteenth century saw the beginning of the retail furnishing shop. The owner was a shop keeper only. He bought from the manufacturer everything he sold. This included, furniture, looking glasses, carpets, wallpapers, lighting fittings, grates, fenders, etc. The only evidence of work on the premises was the upholsterer's shop.

c. 1825 BERNARD FALK, *Turner, the Painter, His Hidden Life*. 1938. Reference to J. M. W. Turner's house, 46a Queen Anne St., Marylebone (now No. 23), where he lived from 1812.

Dirt, an inch thick, lay on the mantel pieces; the unswept carpets, bought second-hand, were as grey as they were evil smelling. In places, owing to damp, the faded and begrimed wall coverings were peeling off. . . .

PALMER'S

Patent Paper-hanging Printing Press.

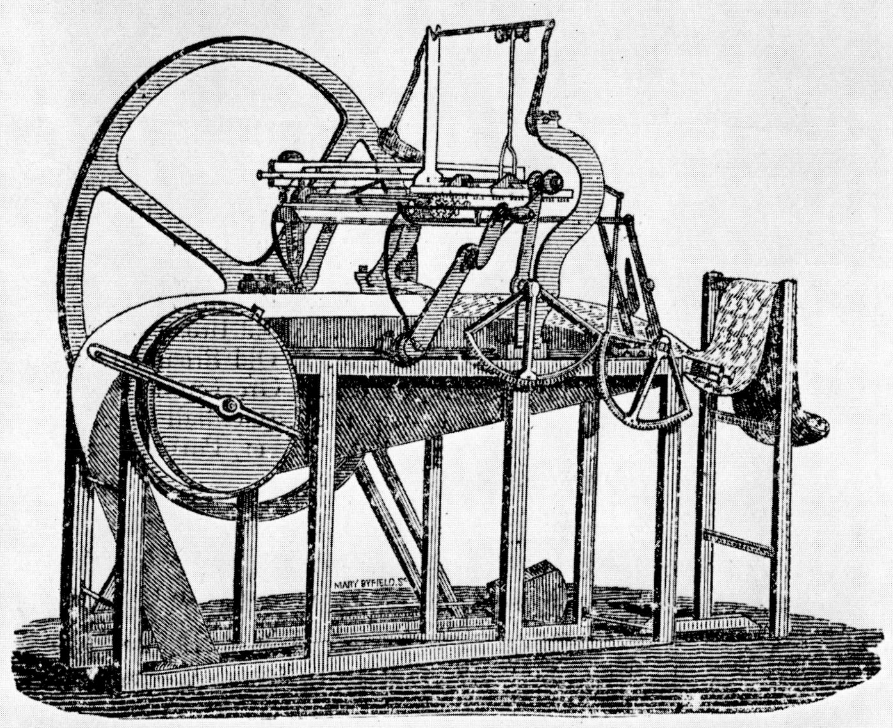

PAPER-HANGING MANUFACTORY,

172, *Bishopsgate Street Without, London.*

WM. PALMER, Paper-hanging Manufacturer, has always on sale, or will make to order, Paper Hangings of the best quality and workmanship, and modern patterns,

AT THE FOLLOWING LOW PRICES.

2½d per Yard and upwards.
6d per yard and upwards for Satin Papers.
Blended Colour Papers, flock and metal, and the richest leafage Papers, at prices in proportion.

Patterns sent for inspection to any part, and Men employed to hang Paper, &c.

Regular sets of Patterns may be had by the trade, but it is expected that 20s. or 30s. to include the Metal Patterns, will be paid for them, which sum will be returned when 20*l.* or more shall have been received for Goods sold.

53 Advertisement issued by an early 19th century manufacturer showing a form of mechanism in use about this time for printing wallpaper

54 One panel of a series 'The Twelve Months of the Year' designed by Fragonard Fils. Hand printed wallpaper by Dufour, Paris, 1808

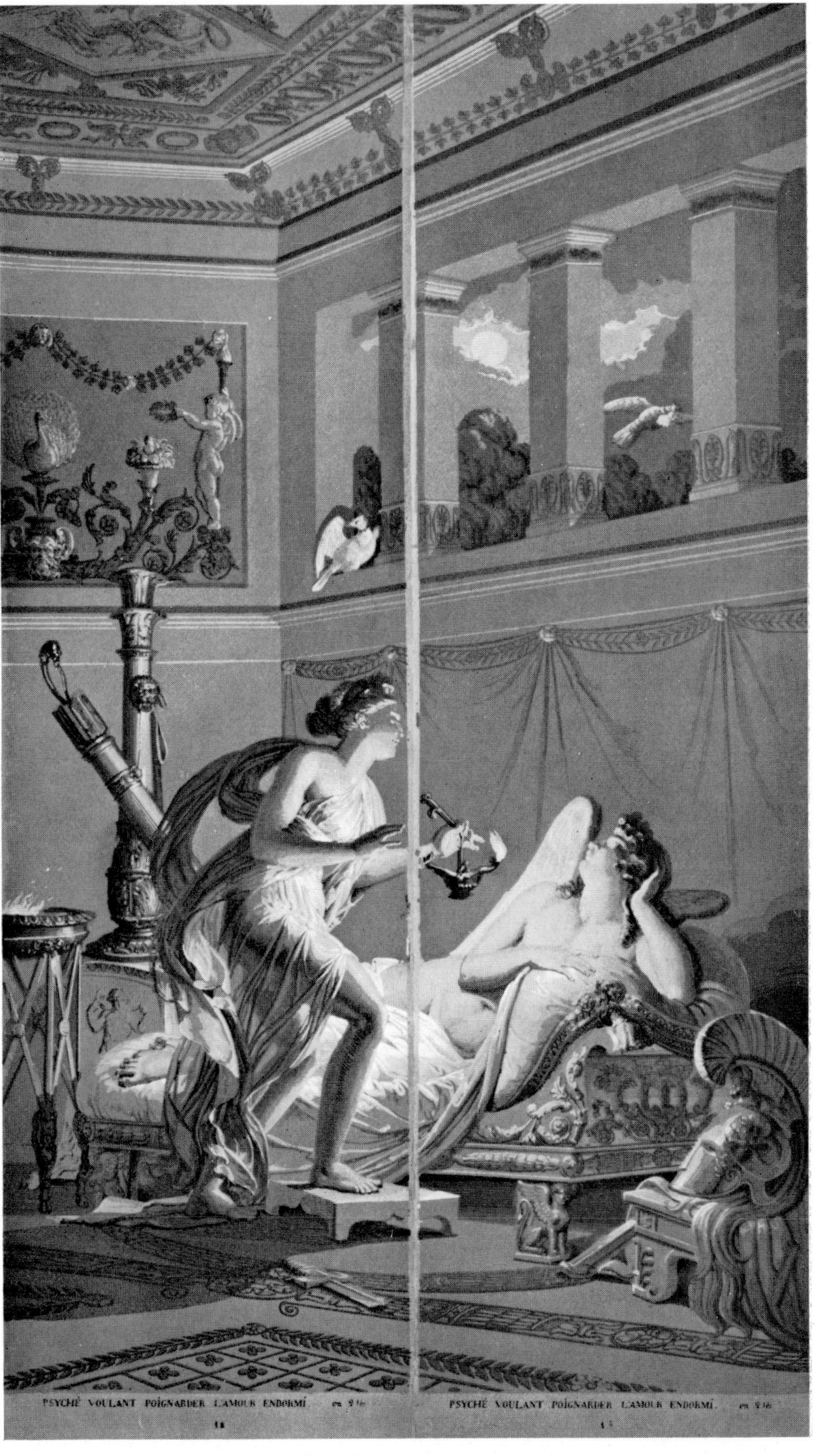

55 Two panels of the French hand printed scenic wallpaper. 'Les Amours de Psyche' printed by Dufour, Paris, *c*.1820. (*See* 1936 André Carlhian)

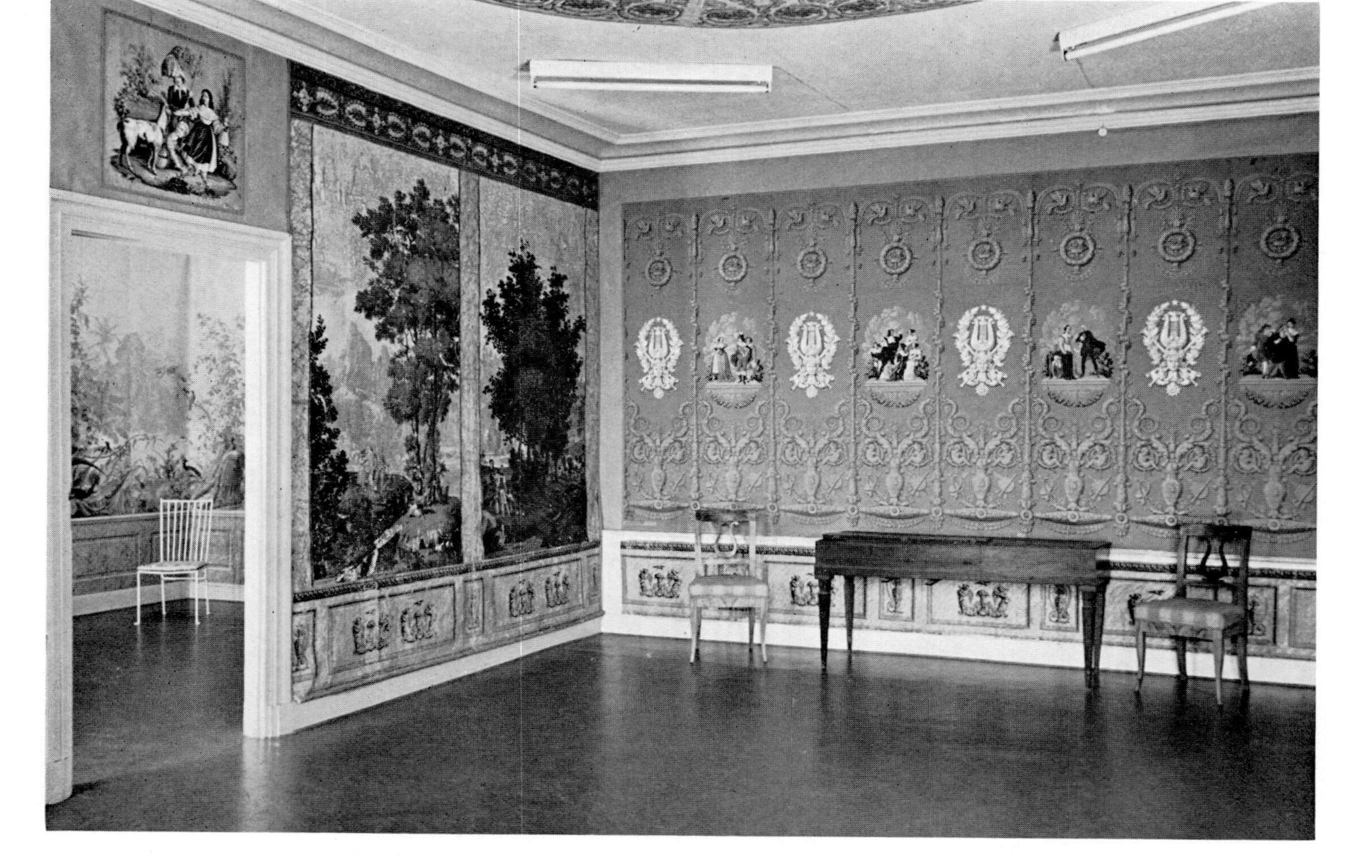

56 A room in the German Wallpaper Museum, Wilhelmshöehe Schloss, Kassel, showing on the wall at the rear a French hand printed wallpaper of the early 19th century. (*See* 1950 Catalogue of the Kassel Museum)

1826 REV. SYDNEY SMITH (of Foston). Writing to his wife from Paris, April 26:

Dearest Kate. I went yesterday into a great upholsterer's shop. Nothing can exceed the magnificence and beauty of the furniture. Their papers are most beautiful so that I think I shall bring some over.

[See 1829 below.]

1827 *The Atlas* (April 29). Reference to Crease's Washable Paperhangings. '*The superiority of these papers consists in the surface being impervious to moisture. . . . Prices are as follows: Bedroom papers 4d.–7d. per yard. Parlour ditto, 7d.–10d.; satin ditto, 11d.–14d.; and Staircase Papers 6d. per yard and upwards.* (See also further particulars about washable papers in R. ACKERMANN's *Repository*. Other makers were: Morton Rule, *c.* 1863; and Lee & Co.'s Oleo Charta, *c.* 1869, etc. Muraline wallpaper (*c.* 1900). [See 1858 below.]

1827 NATHANIEL WHITTOCK, *Decorative Painters' and Glaziers' Guide*. [Does not deal with wallpaper, but useful as one of the early decorators' *vade mecums*, including such items, 'Designs for Decorating Apartments' etc.

1829 Advertisement in London Post Office Directory.

William Palmer Paperhanging Manufacturer, 172 Bishopsgate St. Without. Palmer's Patent Paperhanging Printing Press produces papers 2½d. per yard and upwards: 6d. per yard for satin papers, Blended colour papers, flock and metal, and the richest leafage papers at prices in proportion.

1829 *Memoirs of Rev. Sydney Smith*, by his daughter LADY HOLLAND. A reference to Smith's home at Foston. Extract from a letter written by *a friend:* '*He (Sydney Smith) had no architect but I question whether a more compact, convenient house could be imagined; the drawing room is the colour you covet, the genuine chromium, with a sort of yellow flowering pattern. . . .*' Again, and this time Lady Holland is writing: ' . . . *He (Sydney Smith) threw the whole space of the roof into his bedrooms, coved the ceilings and papered them: and thus they were all airy, gay, cheap and pretty.*'

1830 G. M. YOUNG, *Early Victorian England*. References to Wallpaper.

In 1830 the interior is more Georgian than Victorian. It is not until after the Queen's marriage, and especially after the Exhibition of 1851, that we find the typical mid-Victorian home with its striped or trellised wallpaper.

1830 L. SEB. LE NORMAND, *Manuel du Frabicants d'Étoffes Imprimées et du Fabricant de Papiers Peints* (Paris). Other editions 1832, 1856, etc.

1832 C. T. THACKRAH, *The Effects of Arts, Trades, etc. on the Health.*

Paperstainers suffer chiefly from the rubbing and grinding of the paint. When arsenic or white lead is employed they lose appetite and are affected with severe head-ache. Sickness often results from Prussian blue and arsenic, especially when turpentine is employed. A less immediate but more permanent evil is the impaired vision of the printing department. The blocks which impress the paper, require very accurate adjustment. From this, from the dazzling of the flock and from the application of the eyes to other minute objects, these organs suffer considerably. Dimness of sight incapacitates most men before the age of 50. The men are not addicted to liquor. Indeed the nicety of hand and eye required . . . precludes intemperance.

1832 THOMAS WILLEMENT, writing of the wallpapers used in Charlcote Park, Warwickshire:

The hanging of the flock and metal papers requires very great care. They should have very smooth and stout lining papers, the joints well rubbed down. The effect will be very handsome and well suited to the style of your house. From a quotation in *Country Life*, May 2, 1952.

1833 SIR RICHARD PHILLIPS. *A Dictionary of the Arts of Life and Civilization.* Reference to Paperhangings.

Paperhangings are in pieces of 12 yards long by 20 inches wide and printed by wooden blocks with great rapidity: it is to be regretted that the splendid scenes and varied colours of French paperhangings are not imitated in England.

1835 *Fourteenth Report of the Commissioners of Inquiry into Excise Establishment—Regulations under which Duties on Stained Paper are Charged and Collected.* (Copy in the Library, H.M. Customs & Excise.) This report of 186 pages of closely printed matter is most informative as to the state of the wallpaper industry at this date: verbatim reports of witnesses' statements, methods of collecting tax, French competition, etc. A short abstract was published in *Potters of Darwen*, A. V. SUGDEN and E. A. ENTWISLE, 1939. *There are 108 licensed paper-stainers in England, 2 in Scotland, 46 in Ireland. . . .*

1835 JANE MARCETT. *Willy's Stories for Young Children*, (Longman Rees).

He then went into another room where a man was pasting and hanging up a plain paper. It was of a pretty green colour; but Willy did not like it because it had no flowers on it. 'Stop a little,' said the man, 'and I shall paste up some pretty flowers.' And he saw a girl cutting out some paper in one corner of the room; and he went up to her and saw her cut out some beautiful garlands of flowers; and when they were all cut out, he thought they looked more like real flowers than those painted on the paper; and the paperhanger pasted them up for a border all round the top of the walls next the ceiling and another row of flowers he pasted round the bottom of the room, and the green paper covered all the wall between the two borders.

Many other books of this type providing entertainment and instruction for children published at this time. [See CAROLINE HALSTEAD, 1846, etc].

1836 LUKE HERBERT, *Engineers' and Mechanics' Encyclopaedia.*

Elephant size hand made paper (28″ × 23″) is used almost exclusively for the manufacture of paperhangings, being joined together and printed on.

1836 Repeal of the Duty on wallpaper 'printed, painted or stained'.

1836 *Select Committee on Art and Principles of Design.* (London.) Minutes of Evidence (August 16), p. 193: '. . . *how many pattern drawers* (wallpaper designers) *are there in the metropolis? I should say they did not exceed twelve. . . .*' etc. Interesting information on current wallpaper styles.

57 English hand printed border, peacock feathers and flowers, *c.*1800, from the Octagonal Room, Mount Clare, Roehampton

58, 59, 60 English hand printed borders of classic design, *c.*1820–30

61 Bandbox covered with American hand printed wallpaper, *c.*1820 (Cooper Union Museum, New York)

1837 NATHANIEL WHITTOCK. *The Complete Book of Trades.* Reference under 'Stationer':

This trade bears some affinity to the Papermaker, Printer and Parchment maker besides which the Stationer also branches off into the Law Stationer, the Paper-stainer and Paperhanging maker.

Under 'Paperhanging Printer': *The apprentice fee is from £10–£30, and the capital required to start in business £100–£300.*

1838 W. A. CHATTO and JOHN JACKSON, *Treatise on Wood Engraving.* References to J. B. Jackson's printing by chiaro oscuro methods.

1838 François Bissonnet of France claimed to have invented a wallpaper printing machine, operated manually, which printed one or two colours. [See Études de l'Exposition de 1867.]

1839 Patent No. 8302. Harold Potter (of Darwen, Lancs.) Printing Calicoes and other Fabrics. (A very important patent.) [See also 'Potters of Darwen' 1939].

. . . And my said Invention further consists in the application and use of engraved or cut or figured copper, or other metal rollers for printing paperhangings, and by means of these metal rollers I am enabled to produce patterns shewing a delicacy of light and shade which cannot be had by block printing.

1839 JOHN GREGORY CRACE, 'The History of Paperhangings'. A Paper read to the Royal Institute of British Architects, (February). Published in the Society's *Journal.* Printed in full with Notes by A. V. SUGDEN and E. A. ENTWISLE (privately), in 1939. [See also 1939.]

1839 *Mechanics' Magazine*, Vol. 31. Excerpts from J. G. CRACE's Lecture to the R.I.B.A. first published in this Journal. [See above].

1839 Art Union (London). Occasional articles on wallpaper.

A few years ago, our neighbours, the French, were greatly inferior to us in the manufacture of paperhangings but now through the non-employment of artistical skill on our part and the great exertions to obtain excellence which have been made theirs, we find ourselves considerably in the back ground. Machinery will not do all.

1839 TALLIS'S *London Street Views.* Advertisement in Cheapside Section.

J. Thompson, 124 Cheapside and 386 Oxford Street, calls public attention to the great reduction in paperhangings. Rooms may now be papered for less than they can be stencilled. A good sized room may now be papered for 5/-. Bedroom papers from ½d. per yard; Parlours in every variety of colours from 1d. to 2d.; Satin papers 3d.; Crimson Flock and Metal 3d.

1839 Address spoken at the reopening of Marylebone Theatre by Henry Gordon (May 20).

Reform the boxes and extend the Pit; Make every place for every person fit: Paint, paper, cushion, renovate, renew; Get able actresses and actors too. . . .

1840 FLEURY-CHAVANT, *Le dessinateur du papier peints.* (Henri Clouzot suggests this book was published about this date.)

1840 *Penny Magazine.* Amusing article on 'intellectual' wallpapers.

1840 *Magazine of Science* (May 13), p. 340. See Manufacture of Paperhangings. (In this article no mention is made of the new method of machine printing, e.g. Potter's Patent of 1839. Though there is a reference to Archer & Taverner's machine for mechanically handling the printing blocks. Not a very practical machine, however.)

1840 An article dated about 1890 in an American Journal, *The Painters' Magazine.* The author, R. N. HUNTER describes wallpaper styles of the 1840 period.

> *Wallpaper, in its effort to compete with the expert fresco painter and decorator, had to produce the equal of hand painted decorations, panelled drawing rooms with elaborate details of light and shade mouldings, cornices, centrepieces, columns, capitals, etc. All these details were exquisitely printed on wallpaper, and required the services of the most expert paperhangers not only to place properly the mouldings and ornaments in their true relation for light and shade effects, but to hang the extra wide and plain tinted panels without soiling the surface. . . . Incidentally, the first cut-out borders were introduced at this time and were known as scalloped borders. The paperhanger of that time would depend upon his wife or his children to cut out these borders, or the ladies in the family of his customers would take special pride and delight in doing this part of the important work of decorating the home, and in every case it was exquisitely done.*

c. 1840 EDGAR ALLAN POE. An Essay entitled 'Philosophy of Furniture' published in *The World Classics,* Oxford University Press, 1912. Very interesting, and one of the earliest works to be written on interior decoration from a literary point of view. Poe describes the attributes of carpets, curtains, illumination of rooms, mirrors, American taste or the lack of same, and colour schemes. Of wallpapers he has this to say:

> *The walls are prepared with a glossy paper of a silvery grey tint, spotted with small arabesque devices of a fainter hue of the prevalent crimson. Many paintings relieve the expanse of the paper . . . the tone of each is warm, but dark. There are no 'brilliant effects'.* Repose *speaks in all. Not one is of small size . . . etc.*

1841 A. W. N. PUGIN, *True Principles of Pointed or Christian Architecture.* Contains fugitive references to wallpaper including the following:

> *. . . what are termed Gothic pattern papers for hanging walls, where a wretched caricature of a pointed building is repeated from the skirting to the cornice in curious fashion, door over pinnacle and pinnacle over door. This is a great favourite with hotel and tavern keepers.*

1842 KRÜNITZ, DR. JOHANN GEORG, *Oek-technologische Encyklopädie,* Berlin.

1843 GEORGE DODD, *Days at the Factories,* p. 7. '*Floor-cloth and paper-hangings are London manufactures, carried on in large premises and by a routine of processes very similar throughout.*' Unfortunately a day at a paperstaining factory is not included in this book.

62 Drawing by a contemporary artist of Whiteland Works (Eckhardt Brothers), Chelsea, *c.*1820

SCOTT, CUTHBERTSON, & CO.,

MANUFACTURERS OF PAPER-HANGINGS

OF EVERY DESCRIPTION,

WHITELANDS, CHELSEA, LONDON, S.W.

Messrs. SCOTT, CUTHBERTSON, & Co. respectfully invite the attention of the Trade to their Large Collection of Decorations in every Style; and especially to their New Description of

PAPER-HANGINGS IN RELIEVO,

SUITABLE FOR

DINING AND DRAWING ROOMS, HALLS AND STAIRCASES.

AN EXTENSIVE ASSORTMENT ALWAYS KEPT IN STOCK.

63 An advertisement of 1862 issued by Scott, Cuthbertson & Co., successors of the above firm

64 English hand printed wallpaper of Gothic type about 1830–40

(1)

Your Honorary Secretary having kindly suggested to me that a History & description of the manufacture of Paperhangings might prove interesting to you, I have endeavoured to the best of my ability to comply with his request, and, at the same time, have introduced some account of the earlier decorations whose place they have now so generally supplied —

Paperhangings are of comparatively modern origin and although they are of such consequence both from the present extent of the manufacture and —

65 Holograph opening page of J. G. Crace's Lecture on *The History of Paperhangings*, 1839

66 Portrait of Henry Fourdrinier, associated with the invention of the machine which produced paper in endless lengths. From the *Illustrated London News*, 1854

67 John Gregory Crace. Decorator and Juror of the Great Exhibition of 1851. (See *Journal of the Royal Society of Arts*, 1857, and John Gregory Crace, 1839)

1843 C. H. SCHMIDT, *Die Papier-Tapeten-Fabrikation mit Figurentafeln* (B.M. Copy 'mislaid' August, 1959).

1843 CHARLES DICKENS, *Martin Chuzzlewit*, Chapter 8. (Chapman & Hall, London.) '*. . . it had not been papered or painted, hadn't Todger's within the memory of man*'. Chapter 9 (reference the Drawing Room at Todger's). '*. . . it was floor-clothed all over, and the ceiling including a great beam in the middle, was papered*'. [Other Dickens references below].

1844 (Reminiscences of Georgiana Caroline Sitwell.) *Two Generations*, SIR OSBERT SITWELL (1940).

> *We always spent the hour before dinner in my mother's bedroom formerly—as now again—used as an upstairs drawing room. At that time it was hung with old fashioned prints, the wallpaper was brownish white with leaves upon it, the great bow window overlooking the lawn and park had, like the bed, curtains of crimson moreen, and the carpet was covered with bunches of large peonies.*

1844 *Letters and Memorials of Jane Welsh Carlyle*. Longmans, 1883. Letter No. 1, p. 292: '*The painter, preparatory to the paperer . . . has kept me expecting him until now. . . .*' [See also 1852 and 1858.]

1844 MAWER COWTAN. A Lecture read before The Decorative Art Society (October 9), published in the Society's *Proceedings*, also in *The Builder*, Vol. 2, etc.

> *If we cast our eyes towards the French as our principal competitors we find that the methods in practice here are precisely the same as they have in use: that in the mechanical branches we are superior, and the colours we employ are far more durable; that at one time we equalled their productions of the present day, and the only difference that exists is our want of proper artists, and of course, the want of proper instructors to educate them for the profession.*

1844 *Exposition de l'Industrie Française. Rapport du Jury Centrale, Sec: VI, Papier Peints*, Vol. 3, p. 337.

1845 *The Magazine of Science and School of Arts*, Vol. VI. Reference to paper-hangings, pp. 46, 234, 261, 304, etc. Not very important, but there is another reference on p. 340 of a volume uncertain, which is quite full.

> Extract from Vol. VI: . . . *for paperhangings being manufactured of size colours have, in artificial light especially, a crudity and chalky effect that generally renders them obstrusive and inharmonious.*

1846 CAROLINE A. HALSTEAD, *Investigations, or Travels in the Boudoir*. 3rd Edn. (Contains, under a chapter entitled 'Modern Paperhangings', an edifying account of their manufacture.)

> *How many young persons . . . are totally unacquainted with the origin, history or progress into general use of the most ordinary articles with which they are surrounded: articles which are so essential however to our enjoyment that their absence would convert the most elegant apartment into a hermit's cell, and give to the most cheerful abode an appearance of desolation that would at once dissipate that peculiar air of comfort and domestic luxury, which renders an Englishman's fireside proverbial among foreigners and* HIS HOME *the pride and delight of every true Briton's heart.*

1847 *Dictionary of Science, Literature and Art*, W. T. BRANDE (short entry under 'Paperhangings').

This important and elegant substitute for the ancient hangings of tapestry or cloth came into use about 200 years ago: the manufacture has undergone a gradual succession of improvements, and has now reached a high state of beauty and perfection.

1847 *Journal of Eugène Delacroix*, under date October 9, 1849, DELACROIX writes:

I saw a Chinese wallpaper when I was at Maigret's house . . . Maigret told us that we have nothing to equal their skill in producing fast colours. . . . The wallpaper is comparatively cheap to buy, etc.

1847 D. R. HAY, *The Laws of Harmonious Colouring adapted to Interior Decoration* (Sixth Edition). (W. Blackwood & Sons, Edinburgh). The author, who was a well-known decorator in Edinburgh, includes an informed article on paperhangings—their manufacture and use—and also recounts an interesting story about Sir Walter Scott's instructions for hanging a Chinese paper at Abbotsford. [See 1822, Sir Walter Scott.]

1847-51 WM. MACKENZIE. *National Encyclopaedia or Dictionary of Useful Knowledge*. See under Paperhangings.

. . . a term applied somewhat incorrectly to the stained paper pasted against the walls of an apartment, etc. . . . about 200 years ago, a mode was devised of printing or painting, a pattern on sheets of paper . . . these are paperhangings and they have greatly contributed to the comfort and cleanliness of domestic apartments.

1848 J. L. KINGSLEY and J. P. PIRSSON, editors, *Eureka, or The National Journal of Inventions*, Vols. 1–2 (New York).

1849 GUSTAVE FLAUBERT in his *Travel Notes* mentions seeing the name of a French wallpaper manufacturer painted in black on the Cheops Pyramid in Egypt.

Ascent of the great pyramid Cheops . . . imbeciles have written their names everywhere, 'Buffard, 79 Rue St. Martin, Wallpaper Manufacturer. . . .'

1849 *Journal of Design and Manufacture*, (London, 1849–51). Contains many critical articles on Manufacture, and Design of Wallpaper. Actual samples of wallpaper are included. (Chapman & Hall, 6 Vols.)
(This magazine ran prior to and during the Great Exhibition and was almost wholly devoted to this subject.)

1849 Society of Arts, London. Catalogue of the 'Select Specimens of British Manufactures and Decorative Art' exhibited at the Society's premises (April).

The exhibition of British paperhangings is as complete a representative of the present state of that manufacture as that of the precious metals is in its way: and it encourages the hope that when our Schools of Design are made as efficient as they are capable of being made, the English paper-stainer, instead of generally borrowing his patterns from the French, will be able rather to furnish his rival with examples, as he was accustomed to half a century ago.

68 English hand printed wallpaper panel, *c.*1840–60. Width 22 inches

69 A two-print flock wallpaper designed by A. W. N. Pugin for the Houses of Parliament, *c.*1848

1849 CHARLES DICKENS, *Household Words.* Mr. Crumpet of Clump Lodge, Brixton:

. . . the paper in my parlour contains four kinds of birds of paradise besides bridges and pagodas.

1850 LORD LYTTON, *The Caxtons,* Part 3, Chapter 3. [Pisistratus speaking.] Scene of this Conference, *my own little room, new papered on purpose for my return for good; trellis work paper, flowers and birds, all so fresh, and so new, and so clean, and so gay.*

1850 MRS. C. S. PEEL. *Early Victorian England* (2 Vols.), Vol. 1. Chap. II, 'Homes & Habits', Description of life in a Hertfordshire vicarage:

Our drawing room was papered with a buff and gilt Fleur de Lys patterned paper.

1850 TOMLINSON'S *Encyclopaedia of Arts and Manufactures,* Vol. 2, Part VI, p. 374 (contains long references to Paperstaining).

1850 Victorian wallpapers. [See under 1950, *Decorative Art of Victoria's Era,* FRANCES LICHTEN.]

1850 Mid-Victorian era. [See 1918, ANATOLE FRANCE, *Le Petit Pierre.*]

1851 The year of the Great Exhibition, Hyde Park, London. It is impossible to enumerate the flood of literature that was published during the run of this Exhibition, much of which was descriptive of the various exhibits, including wallpaper. The Catalogue of the Exhibition should be consulted and also the Jury's Reports:

'*Paperhangings form a manufacture of considerable importance carried on in most of the principal cities of Europe, employing many artists and designers and thousands of operatives, consuming also vast quantities of paper, colours, wool and metal. They are important also because they may be made the means of extensively diffusing taste for art; and from the low price of the cheaper kinds, enabling the humblest mechanic to give to his home an air of elegance and comfort.* [See also *Official Illustrated Catalogue Advertizer*; *History of English Wallpaper, 1926,* etc.]

1851 *Official Catalogue of the Great Exhibition.* 4th edn. September 15, 1851. [See pp. 129 *et seq.* for names of exhibitors in Class 26. (Furniture, Upholstery, Paperhangings, etc.]

1851 *The following statistics are given:*

Total Block printing Tables in U.K.	*600*
Workmen Employed	*1,900*
Output in Rolls	*2,300,000*
Av. Value per Roll	*2s. 7d.*

1851 *Exposition Universelle de 1851. Travaux de la Commission Française sur L'Industrie* (Paris, 1855). [See 'Papiers de Tentures'.]

1851 *Cyclopaedia of the Great Exhibition,* 1851. Illustrated. Copious Index. Contains article on paperhangings.

1851 DIGBY WYATT, *Industrial Arts of the Nineteenth Century.* 2 Vols. (London). Articles on current paperhangings of distinction. See Plates XLII; LXXI; XCV; C: with accompanying letterpress. An important source of information on the history of wallpaper.

70 John Woollams & Co.: a well known wallpaper manufacturer of the 19th century. Advertisement from the Official Catalogue of the Great Exhibition of 1851

1851 JOHN TIMBS, *The Year Book of Facts* (published by David Bogue). Contains section on 'Paperstaining' descriptive in a general way of the paperhangings shown at the Exhibition.

1851 M. ZUBER FILS, *The Manufacture of Paperhangings.* Read before The Industrial Society of Mulhausen (August 27).

Towards the end of the last century, about 1780, the manufacture of paperhangings passed from England into France.

1851 Economic Library. *How to Furnish a House and Make it a Home* (London). Chapter on Paperhangings.

Paperhangings are now so cheap that it is almost as little cost to paper a room as to whitewash or colour it, while in appearance it is far superior. A papered room has a comfortable look which no other ordinary material can impart, and the hanging of the paper is not a tedious operation nor unpleasant . . . a safe rule with regard to paperhangings is to choose nothing that looks extravagant or unnatural; no staring pattern or colour, which would only be fit to make caps for May-day Sweeps.

1851 *The Crystal Palace and its Contents.* (B.M. Press Mark 7955 e. 14.)

1851 TALLIS'S *History and Description of the Crystal Palace*, Vol. II, p. 205. Interesting article on wallpaper.

1851 Advertisement. *Official Illustrated Catalogue of the Great Exhibition.*

John Woollams & Co., 69 Marylebone Lane, London. Having been engaged for the last two years in erecting additional works for printing paperhangings by steam cylinder machinery by which they are now enabled to supply a greatly improved article of the cheaper kind of goods. . . .
[See above.]

1851 KNIGHT'S *Cyclopaedia of the Industry of All Nations.* Under Paperhangings:

. . . Progress is however now being made towards the application of cylinder printing. . . . Hitherto these papers have not vied in beauty with block prints, but some of the London houses have recently succeeded in producing beautiful specimens by the cylinder, in which six or eight colours are printed by one passage through the machine. A single machine is capable of printing in one hour 200 pieces of paper, each 12 yds. long; or 18,000 yards per day, etc.

1852 GEORGE DODD, *Curiosities of Industry.* Reference to 'Paper—Its Applications and its Novelties'.

The modern method of cylinder printing is, however, the great step in advance. The making of continuous strips of paper instead of having to paste sheets together, was one notable aid to the paper-stainer; the removal of the Excise duty has been a second; while the use of the cylinder machine has capped those improvements and rendered it possible to make wallpapers at a farthing a yard . . . unless paper ceases to be a material for wall decoration (and there seems no reason why it should cease), the time has come for a little more artistic meaning in the designs, something like an approach to a principle *in decorative patterns. The people, the paper users, will welcome a new infusion of mind in this art. . . .*

1852 JANE WALSH CARLYLE (wife of Thomas Carlyle), writing to her husband (September):

You may calculate on having your bedroom quite ready and the new room in a cleaned-out state, not papered; but really that (the papering) is easily to be borne after what has been to bear.

[See also 1858 below.]

1852 WILKIE COLLINS, *Basil—A Story of Modern Life.*

On my arrival at North Villa I was shown into what I presumed was the drawingroom. Everything was oppressively new. The brilliantly varnished door cracked with a report like a pistol when it was opened; the paper on the walls with its gaudy pattern of birds, trellis work and flowers, in gold, red and green on a white ground looked hardly dry yet; the showy window curtains of white and sky blue, and the still showier carpet of red and yellow seemed as if they had come out of the shop yesterday; the round rosewood table was in a painfully high state of polish.

1852 Exhibition rooms in the new Hermitage building in St. Petersburg hung with plain flock wallpapers.

1853 *Novelties, Inventions and Curiosities in Arts and Manufactures,* (George Routledge & Co., London), 3rd Edn.: Extract: Re new cylinder printing methods.

These improvements have rendered it possible to make wallpapers at a farthing per yard. When we consider that paperhangings used to pay—besides the duty per lb. on all paper—no less than 1¾d. per yard in their capacity as wallpaper, we may cease to wonder at the lowering of price which recent times have witnessed.

The above was also published as KNIGHT'S *Pocket Cyclopaedia.* [See below.]

1853 KNIGHT'S *Pocket Cyclopaedia of Practical and Entertaining Knowledge.* See p. 188, Paperhangings.

Whatever may be said concerning the higher ranks of society paperhangings are certainly a favourable invention in respect to cleanliness, neatness and the comfort of the houses inhabited by the lower grades. . . . Many are the means adopted to give a decorative character to paperhangings . . . some have an appearance imitative of figured or watered silk, produced by passing the paper between slightly heated rollers which have the requisite design engraved upon them, etc. . . .

1854 JAMES ARROWSMITH, *Paperhangers' and Upholsterers' Guide* (London). Extract (page 5): *I am able to remark that at the beginning and up to the middle of last century, papered rooms were only to be here found in the houses of the opulent . . . and judging from the papers I have had to remove to replace with others, those I find have large bold scrolls, plain and embossed, generally in blue on a soft drab ground.*

1854 *Handbook of the Royal Panopticon of Science and Art,* London, pp. 80–81. Brief reference to Paperhangings, Advertisements, etc.

71 Hand-made wallpaper by Hinchliff & Co., Chelsea. Flock and gold on slightly embossed white satin ground. From an actual sample in *The Journal of Design and Manufactures*, June 1849

72 Probably English machine printed wallpaper, *c*.1850.
Width 22 inches, about 12–14 colours

1854 CHARLES DICKENS, *Hard Times*, Chapter 1.

Gradgrind: . . . *Now let me ask you boys and girls, would you paper a room with representations of horses?*

1854 CHARLES KNIGHT, *Paperhangings for Wall Decoration.*

1855 ANTHONY TROLLOPE, *The Warden*, Chapter 8. Reference to the well-furnished breakfast parlour at Plumstead Episcopi.

. . . at any rate it was not without ample consideration that those thick, dark, costly carpets were put down; those embossed but sombre papers hung up . . .

1856 OWEN JONES, *The Grammar of Ornament*, Folio, (Illustrated). Includes 37 propositions on the 'general principles of the arrangement of form and colour in architecture and the decorative arts'.

I have endeavoured to show that the future progress of Ornamental Art may be best secured by engrafting on the experience of the past the knowledge we may obtain by a return to Nature for fresh inspiration. To attempt to build up theories of art, or to form a style, independently of the past, would be an act of supreme folly. It would be at once to reject the experience and accumulated knowledge of thousands of years. On the contrary, we should regard as our inheritance all the successful labours of the past, not blindly following them, but employing them simply as guides to find the true path.

(Also contains a bibliography on each section of decorative styles discussed).

1856 *Notes and Queries* (letter from JAMES KNOWLES, July). Reference to trial of Herman Schinkel of Delft, printer, who in 1568 was accused of publishing books inimical to the Catholic faith. His defence was that these had been printed by his servant in his absence, but he (Schinkel) decided eventually to print roses and stripes on the back of the paper to paper attics with. [See 1568 above.]

1856 SEBASTIEN LE NORMAND, *Nouveau Manuel Complet du Fabricant d'Étoffes Imprimées et du Fabricants de Papiers Peints.* Nouvelle édition par le Colonel Vergnaud, Paris. [See also 1830.]

1856 WILKIE COLLINS. Book of Short Stories, *After Dark*, includes one, 'The Stolen Letter'. Searching for the letter the narrator has one clue to work on, viz., '5 along, 4 across', and tries unsuccessfully to apply this clue to the pattern of the wallpaper which contained 'pillars of trellis work and flowers enclosing a plain green ground, only four pillars along the wall and only two across'.

1857 PAPERMAKING. *Journal of the Society of Arts* (February 27), p. 237. 'The Origin of the Machine for Making Endless Paper, and its Introduction into England.' A Letter from JOHN GAMBLE.

1857 ROBERT FORTUNE, *Residence among the Chinese.* Reference to Chinese mural decorations.

He now led me into a nicely furnished room, . . . its walls were hung with pictures of flowers, birds and scenes of Chinese life, . . . etc.

1857 M. E. CHEVREUL, (Director of Gobelin's Dye Works), *The Laws of Contrast of Colour*. Probably first translation. Includes section on paperhangings with particular reference to colours used. [See Second Edition, 1872.]

1857 GUSTAVE FLAUBERT, *Madame Bovary*.

Wallpaper of a canary yellow, relieved along its upper edge by faded swags of flowers, trembled perpetually over its whole extent because the canvas on which it was hung had been imperfectly stretched.

1857 THOMAS HUGHES, *Tom Brown's School Days*, Chapter 5. Description of one of the Rugby studies.

The walls were wainscoted half way up, the wainscot being covered with green baize, the remainder with a bright patterned paper.

1857 J. MUNSELL, *Chronology of Paper and Papermaking* (Albany, *N.Y.*)

1640. The manufacture of wallpaper was begun about this time, as a substitute for the ancient hangings of tapestry, or cloth. They reached a high state of beauty and perfection.

(There are a number of similar references under other dates).

1858 Washable Wallpapers. (Abbrev. Patent Specification 1879).

Wallpapers covered with coating of varnish, formalin, casein clay, casein mica, or synthetic resins. An early inventor of these was F. H. Whiteman, who in 1858 was granted a patent No. 1272 for treating paperhangings with a solution of borax and shellac.

[See 1827 above.]

1858 WATERSTON'S *Cyclopaedia of Commerce*.

Exports of British made paperhangings at this time, 14,778,375 yards; value £74,649. Largest quantities went to Australia, U.S.A. and British North America.

1858 *The Builder* (July 3).

An intelligent person who has been for about forty years connected with the paperstaining business says that many of the common wallpapers were printed on old newspapers for the purpose of avoiding the duties.

(Subsequent numbers of this journal also deal at intervals with wallpaper.)

1858 From J. L. HALLIDAY'S *Mr. Carlyle—My Patient*. Thomas Carlyle to his wife with reference to their former house Craigenputtock:

Our old dining room is now papered in a flaming pattern; your old paper is on the other two rooms, dim like the fading memories.

1858 CHARLES KNIGHT, *Pictorial Gallery of Arts*, 2 Vols. In Vol. 1, p. 178, there is a full account of paperstaining, history and practice, as well as facetious criticism of wallpaper design.

1859 *Dictionnaire Universel Théorique et Pratique du Commerce*, etc. (Paris). Libraire de Guillaumin et Cie, Vol. 2. Article, 'Papier Peints', by L. WOLOWSKI, pp. 971–7.

73 Cheap English machine printed wallpaper illustrated in *The Journal of Design and Manufactures*, April 1849

74 Another English machine printed wallpaper, *c*.1852

75 An elegant floral panel produced by a French manufacturer, *c.*1850. Hand printed and probably used in the form of panels on either side of a doorway or window

76 English wallpaper, *c*.1850, hand printed throughout in many tones of russet, gold and brown. Width 22 inches

77 English machine printed wallpaper depicting the harbour of Cronstadt during the Crimean war. 22 inches wide

78 Another English pictorial machine printed wallpaper, *c.*1870, from an old house at Worthy Park, near Winchester

1859 *Universal Decorator*, edited by FRANCIS BENJAMIN THOMPSON (George Vickers, London), 3 Vols. Articles on wallpaper by William Gibbs. References to paperhangings: Vol. 2, Part X, a resumé of an article from BECHSTEIN'S *History of Inventions.* Part XI, article on paperstaining, Part XIX, 'Ornamental Paperhanging'.

1859 EDMUND GOSSE, *Father and Son,* Chapter 8. Published October, 1907. Reference to 1859.

Neither of them had ever been in our drawing room since it was furnished and I thought that each of them noticed how smart the wallpaper was.

1860 *The English Cyclopaedia—A New Dictionary of Universal Knowledge.* Conducted by CHARLES KNIGHT. The 1860 Volume contains under 'Paperhangings' a long and accurate account of the history and progress of the industry. This includes a reference to the 1857 Enquiry by the House of Lords into the 'Sale of Poisons', the wallpaper aspect of which (arsenic) was raised by a Dr. A. S. Taylor. There are also references to Fiscal Changes, Printing of Oak Grain Papers, Design, etc.

c. 1860 IVAN S. TURGENEV'S *First Love.* (One of the author's short stories.)

. . . The house we had taken was a wooden building with pillars and had two small, low lodges. In the lodge on the left was a tiny factory for the manufacture of cheap wallpaper. Occasionally I used to wander over to it and watch a dozen or so village boys, lean, tousle-headed, with pinched faces, in long, greasy smocks, as they jumped on to wooden levers and forced them down on to the square blocks of the presses and in this way by the weight of their shrunken bodies, stamped the brightly coloured patterns on the paper.

1860 DR. ANDREW URE'S *Dictionary of Arts, Manufactures and Mines* (Fifth Edition). See Vol. 3 'Paperhangings'. A detailed and very interesting account of the manufacture of wallpaper at this date. The making of Flock papers (papiérs tontisse) described in great detail. No mention of machine made papers. Interesting account of papier maché manufacture, paper-making and in Vol. 1, calico printing.

(re Arsenic). *The use of arsenic in paperhangings has of late* (*1859*) *been the subject of much discussion, and many absurd statements have been made respecting its injurious effects. . . . All that has been said about the volatilisation of the arsenic under the influence of the gas used in the rooms betrays the ignorance of those who have written on the subject.*

1860-70 From *Le Second Empire* (Souvenirs d'un Contemporain), by d'OCTAVE AUBRY. (Marigny et Joly, Caen, 1935.) Reference to dresses made of wallpaper:

La crinoline fut aussi la prétexte d'inventions bizarres: je veux parler des robes en papier peint. Pour ne pas être taxé de vouloir rivaliser avec M. de Crac, je copie, dans une revue du temps ce passage dont on ne pourra soupçonner l'authenticité: 'Voici, en fait de toilette une fantaisie originale, dont la mode va s'emparer. Cette invention n'a qu'un tort: le bon marché tort grave a une époque au rien n'est beau que ce qui est cher. Il s'agit de robes en papier peint. Sur une crinoline ad hoc, recouverte d'une forte toile, on colle une étoffe de papier élastique, imperméable et résistant. Da la sorte on peut avoir au prix d'une robe d'indienne, une robe d'argent, une robe moirée, variée a l'infini de nuances et de dessins. Et combien de temps durera une telle robe? Six mois, prétend M. Louis Fiquier dans son Année Scientifique. *Ne comptons que sur huit jours: ce sera déjà beau. Que de robes et des plus belles, ne sont mises que trois ou quatre fois! Désormais, une élegante pourra acheter sa robe au rouleau et les jeunes danseuses, commes les douairieres, feront véritablement tapisseries. Les tapissiers remplaceront les coutourières; ces heureux industriels passeront tel jour et à telle heure, pour renouveler la tenture du salon et la toilette de Madame*'.

1861 *Our English Home—Its Early History and Progress.* (J. H. and James Parker, Oxford and London.) Reference to Introduction of Paperhangings, p. 174.

1861 JOHN STEWART, *Art Journal* (January, February and April). 'French and English Paperstaining'—*the book of wallpaper*, 1954, quotes this article at some length.

The first reason why the French makers are more successful is that they conduct their business in a far more liberal and enlightened spirit.

1861 *Manchester Daily Examiner and Times* (March 19 and 26). 'French and English Paperstaining'. A reply to criticism of English paperstaining in the *Art Journal*—see above.

1862 *Illustrated London News* (June 7 and July 5). 'Surface Decoration wrought by Block Printing'. Interesting sidelight on some of the wallpapers exhibited at the International Exhibition of this year. Wallpapers were not infrequently commented upon in this journal.

1862 DR. CHRISTOPHER DRESSER, *The Art of Decorative Design* (Day & Son, London) Illustrated.

1862 Children's Employment Commission. Government Report on visits to various paperstaining factories. A most important source of information on manufacturing practice at this date. Extracts are included in the privately printed book *Potters of Darwen*, 1939.

1862 International Exhibition. Official Catalogue of the Industrial Section (printed for H.M. Commissioners by Truscott, Son & Simmons, London). Class 30, Sub Class B, List of Wallpaper Manufacturers exhibiting.

1862 International Exhibition (London). Jurors' Reports on Class XXX Furniture, Paperhangings, etc.

1862 *The Art Journal*, Illustrated Catalogue of the International Exhibition.

1862 W. F. EXNER, *Geschichte des Papiers* (Vienna).

1863 J. B. WARING, *Masterpieces of Industrial Art.* Reference International Exhibition of 1862. (3 Vols. Folio.) References to wallpaper.

1863 WATERSTON'S *Cyclopaedia of Commerce.* Contains statistical information relating to wallpaper.

79 English hand printed wallpaper in Gothic style, *c*.1860, found recently in a house in Sittingbourne, Kent

80 English 'sanitary' printed wallpaper depicting Charles Dickens' characters. Probably 1860–70 period

1865 CHARLES DICKENS, *Our Mutual Friend,* II, IX. (Chapman & Hall, London).

a young lady . . . who was better worth staring at than the best of wall-papering.

1865 ANGUS DAVIDSON, *Edward Lear,* (John Murray, London, 1938). Apropos Lear's furnished lodgings on the Promenade des Anglais, Nice, at this date:

The (carpet and) papers are so extremely damnable that they resemble large flights of red and blue and green parrots with roses and mustard pots interspersed so that I had to buy £4 worth of brown Holland to cover them up or I should have gone blind or mad.

1865 *The Art Journal.*

Machinery, at least for the present, seems to have its bounds and these do not include paperstaining. Fortunes have been spent here in groping after something to supersede the skilled workman in this walk but hitherto without success, and the conviction among all practical men is that all the anticipations, whether for good or evil, respecting the introduction of machinery into paper-staining are now fainter and feebler than at any period during the last 20 years. Those who have machines continue to use them regularly or casually, but it has been found that for all but the commonest class of goods the supposed speed or accuracy of register does not compensate for other deficiencies and after all, good hand block papers are more and more securing the best markets.

81 Typical arrangement of composite wallpaper panels popular during the 19th century

1865 PETER PARLEY'S ANNUAL. Article relating to Robert Horne, paper-hanging manufacturer, of London.

1865 *Manchester City News and Salford Hundred Advertizer* (May 27 and June 3). 'Lancashire Workshops. C. & J. G. Potter, Papermakers and paper-stainers, Darwen, Lancs.'

1866 *The Boy's Book of Trade*, (George Routledge & Sons). See Chapter on 'The Paperstainer'.

1866 FIODOR M. DOSTOEVSKY, *Crime and Punishment*. Wallpaper is mentioned more than once, and Raskolnikoff is made to hide stolen jewellery behind the torn wallpaper in his room.

1866 ALPHONSE DAUDET, *Lettres de mon Moulin*. One of the stories in this book (Les Vieux) describes two anxious old people who have not seen their son for a number of years. A friend of their son who visits them is plied with questions about their boy's welfare—they even want to know the colour of his wallpaper. '*Quelle couleur était le papier de sa chambre?*' they ask. '*Il est bleu, madame, bleu clair, avec des guirlandes.*'

1866 *Dictionary of Science, Literature and Art*. (Longmans Green & Co). Under 'Paperhangings':

> *. . . papers are sometimes printed with varnish or size, and gilt or copper leaf applied; or bisulphide of tin* (AURUM MUSIVUM) *is dusted over so as to adhere to the pattern . . . powdered steatite or French chalk, is used as the ground for satin papers the gloss being produced by . . . polishing.*

1867 Official Catalogue of Paris Exhibition (Statistics based on 1861.)

Operatives engaged in Wallpaper Production

	MALES	FEMALES	TOTAL
England and Wales	1,556	399	1955
Scotland	77	38	115
Ireland	96	9	105
	1,729	446	2,175

1867 EUGÈNE LACROIX, *Études sur l'Exposition de 1867* (Paris), p. 183, KOEPPLIN. 'Notice sur la fabrication des papiers peints.'

> *But whilst according full praise to the English for inventing the 20-colour wallpaper printing machine we must not forget the little French machine of François Bissonnet which was worked by hand in 1838 and which rendered immense service to our industry.*

1867 JOSEPH GWILT, F.S.A. *An Encyclopaedia of Architecture*. Revised, W. PAPWORTH. 2 Vols. (Longmans). See Vol. II, paras. 2278, 2291.

> *The walls of a room should always be stripped before the new paper be put up, a process usually shirked, even when charged in the estimate.*

1867 PROSPER POITÉVIN. *Les papiers peints et la papeterie, dans l'Exposition Universelle de 1867*, Vol. 2, p. 438.

1868 B. J. TALBERT, *Gothic forms applied to Furniture, Decorations, etc.*

1868 C. L. EASTLAKE in the 1st Edn. of *Hints on Household Taste:*

> *About fifteen years ago a fashion prevailed of arranging paper in panels round a room and enclosing them with narrow strips of the same material stained and shaded in imitation of wood. This style of decoration had its admirers, but though attractive from its novelty it was false in principle*

and no one need regret that it has fallen into disuse. And in the 4th Edn., 1878. The author expresses a hope:

That a time will arrive when those who are chiefly concerned with the control and management of industrial art in this country will perceive the necessity of meeting a demand which has existed for some time among our art loving public, for improved taste in objects of modern manufacture.

1869 PROF. DR. W. F. EXNER, *Die Buntpapier und Tapeten—Industrie* (Weimar). This book contains a comprehensive description of the wallpaper industry in Austria. Its history, the design aspect, raw materials, manufacture as well as comments on the future of the industry. Its author also published the following books: *Geschichte des Papiers*, Vienna, 1862; and *Die Buntpapier und Tapetenindustrie auf der Pariser Ausstellung*, 1867.

1870 CHARLES TOMLINSON, *Cyclopaedia of Useful Arts and Manufactures.* 9 Vols. Large 8°. Illustrated. Interesting references to wallpaper. Reference under 'Paperhangings' and 'Flock papers'.

The preparation of the flock is as follows: The flock when obtained from the woollen cloth manufacturers is then stove-dried and ground to a fine powder. This is further prepared by sifting to different degrees of fineness in a bolting machine. It is then placed in a large chest or drum whose width and capacity are such that the child can draw the printed paper into it by degrees at its full width and sprinkle the flock thereon. When about 7 feet have thus been drawn in the child shuts the lid of the drum and beats with rods on the bottom which is made of tense calf's skin and is elevated 2 ft. from the floor by means of strong supports. This beating raises a cloud of flock inside which, as it subsides, falls uniformly on the paper. The chest is then opened, the paper inverted and lightly tapped to detach loose particles.

1871 *The House Furnisher* (July 1), 'Materials for Wall Decoration—Paperhangings'. Contains long list of contemporary wallpaper manufacturers.

Extract (June 1, Vol. 1, No. 5): . . . *and yet amidst all the error that has prevailed there has never at any time been wanting witnesses for the truth. To those desirous of procuring them it has always been possible with more or less difficulty, to obtain papers such as they ought to be and although the constant production of so many and so great absurdities has had its natural consequences of bringing the entire manufacture into much ridicule and contempt yet the perfect legitimacy and raison d'etre of paperhangings upon correct principles must be unhesitatingly confirmed. Their antiquity, their facility of execution and application, and cheapness of production all speak of them as a legitimate material of decoration and no sham.*

1871 MARIUS VACHON, *Les Arts et les Industries du Papier en France* (1871–94). Contains chapter on 'La Fabrication du Papier Peint à la Machine, à la Planche', etc., and 'Le papier de fantasie'.

1872 Wallpaper Curtains. *International Exhibition Review and Trade Directory*, 1872–3. Interesting reference to this product which was made by Pavy, Pretto and Co., London, indicating that a demand for this article existed about this time. The paper was made from special raw material, printed by wallpaper mills in England or France and then banded, sewn and lined. [See below, 1878, Lady Barker.]

1872 *The Building News* (October 11), 'Wallpapers'. This magazine featured references to wallpaper from this date to the '80's—usually inspired by Jeffrey & Co., Islington.

1872 M. E. CHEVREUL, *The Principles of Harmony and Colours—and their Application to the Arts.* An enlarged and revised edition of this author's work of 1857.

1873 LEO TOLSTOY, *Anna Karenina,* Part VI, Chap. 19. This novel of contemporary Russian life was started by the author this year. Describing a visit to Anna's home:

> . . . *Everything was new, from the French wallpaper to the carpet which covered the whole floor.*

Idem, Part VII, Chap. 25.

> . . . *'You can't imagine how I have come to loathe these rooms,' she remarked. 'There's nothing more awful than these "chambres garnies", they have no individuality, no soul. This clock, the curtains, and worst of all, the wallpapers—they're a nightmare.'*

1874 R. C. KEDZIE, 'Shadows from the Walls of Death'—reference to arsenical wallpapers collected by R.C.K.

1874 *Practical Magazine,* 'Paperstaining'. Interesting article describing the industry at this date and giving a particular description of machine printing at the works of John Allen [sic], Old Ford, London, E.

> *Designs for paperhangings are supplied by ordinary art students, and their production affords a valuable opportunity of exhibiting practical art where that rare faculty exists.*

1874 *The Pictorial World* (September 12), p. 40. Short article on the Manufacture of Paperhangings with a drawing of block printers at work by W. LINTON.

1874-5 WALTER CRANE, *An Artist's Reminiscences* (Methuen & Co., 1907). References to his designs for wallpaper at this date. [See 1894].

1875 G. H. MORTON, *History of Paperhangings.* Comprehensive paper read before the Liverpool Architectural and Archaeological Society (February 10), with a review of other methods of Mural Decoration.

1876 RICHARD REDGRAVE, R.A., *Manual of Design,* No. 6 of the South Kensington Museum Art Handbooks. Reprinted 1887.

> Extract from Section on 'Paper and Other Hangings': *The lately introduced processes of printing paperhangings by such machinery as is used for cotton goods, and of applying many colours from one block, are, we fear, likely to create a style of ornamentation for such fabrics of the most depraved style.*

1876 W. F. LOFTIE, B.A., *A Plea for Art in the House.*

> *In sitting rooms the paper is always a serious subject. I like to see dining rooms painted or panelled especially in town, but the drawing room according to all received traditions, must be papered: and nothing can be more hideous than the majority of London drawing room papers.*

1876 MRS. M. J. LOFTIE, *The Dining Room.* Not in B.M.

1876 MRS. ORRINSMITH, *The Drawing Room, its Decoration.* Not in B.M.

This Fac-Simile is Used as a

SUPPLEMENT TO THE CHICAGO HERALD.

THE DAILY CITIZEN.

J. M. SWORDS,...Proprietor.

VICKSBURG, MISS.

THURSDAY, JULY, 2, 1863.

☞ Mrs. Cisco was instantly killed on Monday, on the Jackson road. Mrs. Cisco's husband is now in Virginia, a member of Moody's artillery, and the death of such a loving, affectionate, and dutiful wife will be a loss to him irreparable.

☞ We are indebted to Major Gillespie for a steak of Confederate beef *alias* meat. We have tried it, and can assure our friends that if it is [illegible] y need [illegible] It is [illegible]

GOOD NEWS.—In devoting a large portion of our space this morning to Federal intelligence, copied from the Memphis Bulletin of the 25th, it should be remembered that the news, in the original truth, is whitewashed by the Federal Provost Marshal, who desires to hood-wink the poor Northern white slaves. The former editors of the Bulletin being rather pro southern men, were arrested for speaking the truth when truth was unwelcome to Yankeedom, and placed in the chain-gang working at Warrenton, where they now are. This paper at present is in duress, and edited by a pink-nosed, slab-sided, toad eating Yankee, who is a lineal descendant of Judis Iscariot and a brother germain of the greatest Puritanical, sycophantic, howling scoundrel unhung—Parson Brownlow. Yet with such a [illegible]

Yankee News from all Points.

PHILADELPHIA, June 21, 2:30, A. M.—The following is all the news of interest in the Washington Star:

Major Brazell, of the United States Volunteers, received intelligence from Fayette county, Penn., this morning that the rebels in heavy force were advancing on Pittsburg via the National Road leading from Cumberland across the Alleghany Mountains. Their pickets had reached Grantsville, Md., thirty-eight miles from Uniontown, Fayette county, Penn., on Wednesday evening last.

It is reported in Washington to-day that two members of Hooker's staff were gobbled up by guerrillas last night in the vicinity of Fairfax.

HARRISBURG, June 20.—Operations were commenced on our side to-day by a portion of a New York cavalry regiment, capturing twenty [illegible] at McConnelsburg, in [illegible]

These will be defended by Union League men, who are being armed by Gen. Schenck. The Union men are confident that the rebels will not be so rash as to attempt a raid in that direction. The disloyal among us are evidently uneasy, and begin to realize that any hostile movement of the rebel army against Baltimore might result disastrously among themselves.

A Herald's special from Monocacy Station, Md., the 21st, says: About 4 o'clock P. M., Major Cole, of the 1st Maryland cavalry, made a gallant dash into Frederick, with forty men driving out the enemy, killing two and capturing one. No loss on our side. Our cavalry passed through the city, and immediately after about 1500 rebel cavalry re-occupied the town.

Rebel cavalry entered Frederick yesterday P. M., about 6 o'clock, and dashed furiously through the city, capturing nine of our men on duty at the signal station, and paroled the invalid soldiers, numbering about sixty.

82 Newspaper printed on wallpaper (facsimile of *The Daily Citizen* (U.S.A.), 1863)

INDUSTRIE DES PAPIERS PEINTS. 333

Fig. 135. — Machine à imprimer les papiers peints en 20 couleurs.

A. — Rouleau de papier à imprimer.
B. — Papier imprimé parcourant le séchoir.
C. — Retour du papier séché.
D. — Robinet de vapeur chauffant le séchoir.

83 Twenty-colour wallpaper printing machine. An illustration from Louis Figuier's book, *Merveilles de l'Industrie*, published in Paris, 1878

1878 LADY BARKER, *The Bedroom and the Boudoir* (Macmillan 'Art at Home' series). Writing of wallpaper curtains: *The curtains made of it are not only a sham but they are generally of very ugly patterns, and hang in stiff ungraceful folds, crackling and rustling with every breath of air, besides being very inflammable.*

1878 LOUIS FIGUIER, *Les Merveilles de l'Industrie* (Illustrated). Les Papiers Peints, Paris. Chiefly relates to Papermaking but includes chapter on Paperstaining. (A very useful book indeed).

Ce n'est pas seulement en France et en Angleterre que la fabrication des papiers peints s'est développée. Établie successivement en Allemagne, en Hollande et en Belgique, elle fut emportée plus tard à Vienne, à Varsovie et en Espagne. La Russie vit un grand établissement impérial s'élèver a Tzarskoe-Selo. Plus tard, vers l'année 1840, les frères Gretchy de Mulhouse, créèrent une belle fabrique de papiers peints à Saint-Pétersbourg, et établirent à Moscow un dépôt de leurs produits.

L'Amérique n'a pas voulu rester complétement tributaire de l'Europe pour cette industrie. Depuis quelques années surtout les fabriques de papiers peints s'y sont multipliées. Dans ces usines tout se fait mécaniquement; l'impression, de même que le foncage et le satinage, se font à la vapeur. Les produits obtenus ont l'avantage du bon marché, mais ils sont inférieurs sous le rapport du goût et de la bonne facture, aux produits similaires des fabriques européennes. Les produits français au contraire, se recommandent par la goût qui préside à leur fabrication. Produire, vite et beaucoup tel est, à coup sûr, le but de tout industriel; mais l'élégance et un certain cachet, gracieux, characterisent toujours les produits français . . . Nos fabricants de papiers peints sont pénétrés de cette parole de Necker: 'Les goût est pour la France le plus adroit de tous les commerces.'

again a reference to the colours used:

La base de la couleur qui sert au foncage (grounding), est le blanc de Bougival, la craie, la céruse ou d'autres substances analogues, réduites en poudre très fine et bien épurées par des lavages. A cette terre, on ajoute une certaine quantité de colle, qui sert à fixer le mélagne sur le papier. Les couleurs sont en poudres ou liquides . . . les ocres: l'outremer (les cendres bleues ou vertes); le bois de Brésil (qui donne le rouge); la gaude, (qui donne le jaune), le bois de campêche (qui produit un beau violet), etc.

(This section is specially detailed).

See also pp. 313–340. The chapter on the Industry deals very fully with the antecedents of wallpapers, e.g., tapestries, leather, etc. It includes references to some of the great French makers and those in this country and describes contemporary types of wallpaper, the colours used and the methods of manufacture.

1878 WILLIAM BLACK, *Macleod of Dare*. (Macmillan, London). 3 Vols., Chapter XLI.

That was the guide she turned to—the woman man, the dabbler in paint boxes, the critics of carpets and wallpapers.

1879 *The Paperhanger, Painter and Grainers' Assistant*. Ken & Co. (Illustrated.) Contains a history of paperhangings of somewhat elementary character.

1879 *J. B. Papworth (Architect). A Brief Record of his Life and Work 1775–1847*, by WYATT PAPWORTH. J. B. P. studied for a year with Sherringham of Great Marlborough St. (the Wedgwood of Paperstainers). Contains short reference to Sherringham and his work at Carlton House, *c*. 1790. [J. B. P. also associated with the Government Enquiry into Design. See 1836 above.]

1880 John Ruskin (apropos Brantwood, Coniston—the writer's home). W. G. COLLINGWOOD'S *The Life of John Ruskin*, Book IV, Chapter VI.

The honoured guest—and all guests are honoured there—after welcome, is ushered up a narrow stair, which betrays the original cottage, into the Turret Room. It had been the 'professor's' until after his illness, and he papered it with naturalistic pansies, to his own taste, and built out at one corner a projecting turret to command the view on all sides.

1880 ARNOLD BENNETT, *The Old Wives' Tale*, (Hodder & Stoughton), Part I, Chapter 1. This book was written in 1907 and deals with the 1880 period.

That corner cupboard of oak inlaid with maple and ebony in a simple border pattern, was typical of the room. It was of a piece with the deep green flock wallpaper, and the tea urn, and the rocking chairs with their antimacassars, and the harmonium in rosewood. . . .

Idem., Chapter 3. *Forget-me-knots on a brown field ornamented the walls of the kitchen.*

1880 *Exposition Universelle Internationale de 1878 à Paris. Rapports du Jury Internationale*. Les Papiers Peints. Groupe III, Classe 22, by M. ISIDORE LEROY.

Papers exhibited in 1855 and 1867 by different makers, and produced by 3,000 or 4,000 blocks were considered exceptional productions and true chef-d'oeuvres of industry. This is no longer the case today, and now quite simply, using fewer blocks, equally beautiful examples can be produced. These are regarded as 'current' products moreover, not exceptional, which makes their appearance all the more interesting. (Trans. from *Rapport du Jury Internationale*).

1880 *British Mail and Journal* of the Chambers of Commerce of the United Kingdom (June 1) describes the wallpaper business of C. & J. G. Potter, Darwen, Lancs., inventors of the Wallpaper Printing Machine.

1880 EMILE ZOLA, *Nana*, Chapter 5. First published February 15, 1880. Describing a theatre dressing room in Paris:

. . . It was a long, ill-built room under the roof, with a garret ceiling and sloping walls. . . . It was papered with a paper at seven sous a roll, with a pattern of roses twining over green trellis work.

1880 REX WHISTLER. Very delightful drawing by this artist depicting a Victorian sitting room with its ornamental wallpaper; published in *The Masque*, Vol. 7. [See 1948].

c. 1880 THOMAS B. ALDRICH in *The Story of a Bad Boy* describes his bedroom at Rivermouth, U.S.A., when he was a boy:

I had never had a chamber all to myself before . . . pretty chintz curtains hung at the window and the pattern of the wallpaper left nothing to be desired. . . . On a gray background were small bunches of leaves, unlike any that ever grew in this world; and on every other bunch perched a yellow bird, pitted with crimson spots, as if it had just recovered from a severe attack of the small pox. . . . There were 268 of these birds in all, not counting those split in two where the paper was badly joined. [This recollection probably belongs to the 1840–50's.]

84 Victorian sitting-room with its ornamental wallpaper. Drawing by Rex Whistler for Sir Osbert Sitwell's film 'A Place of One's Own'. *See* 1948 *The Masque*, a journal edited by Lionel Carter

85 Designed by Owen Jones in 1874. An example of this artist's beautiful if austere sense of design which had a marked influence on later wallpaper designers. (Victoria and Albert Museum)

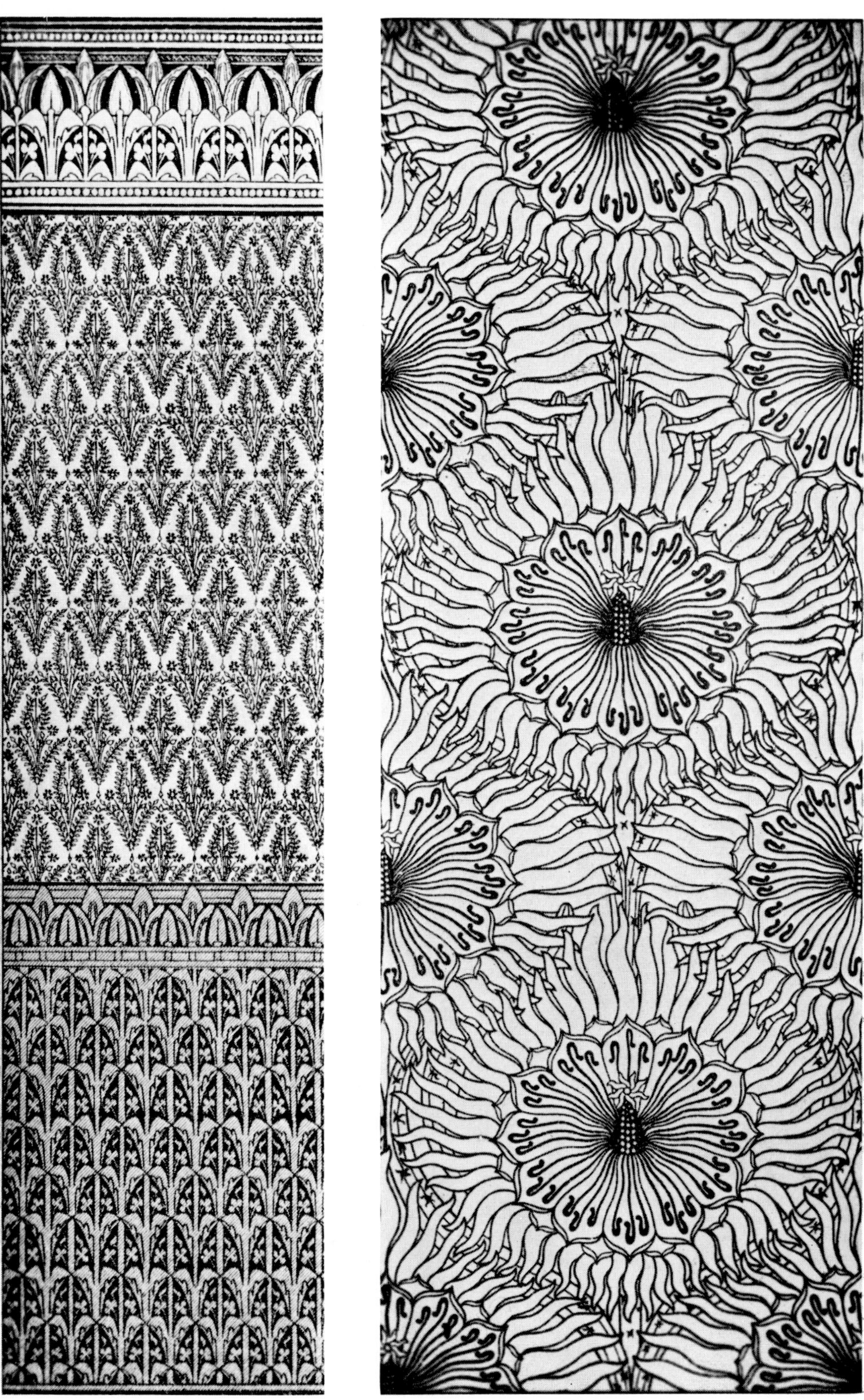

86 Design for frieze, filling and border by Dr. Christopher Dresser, 1874
87 'Cereus': wallpaper designed by C. F. A. Voysey, 1886. (Victoria and Albert Museum)

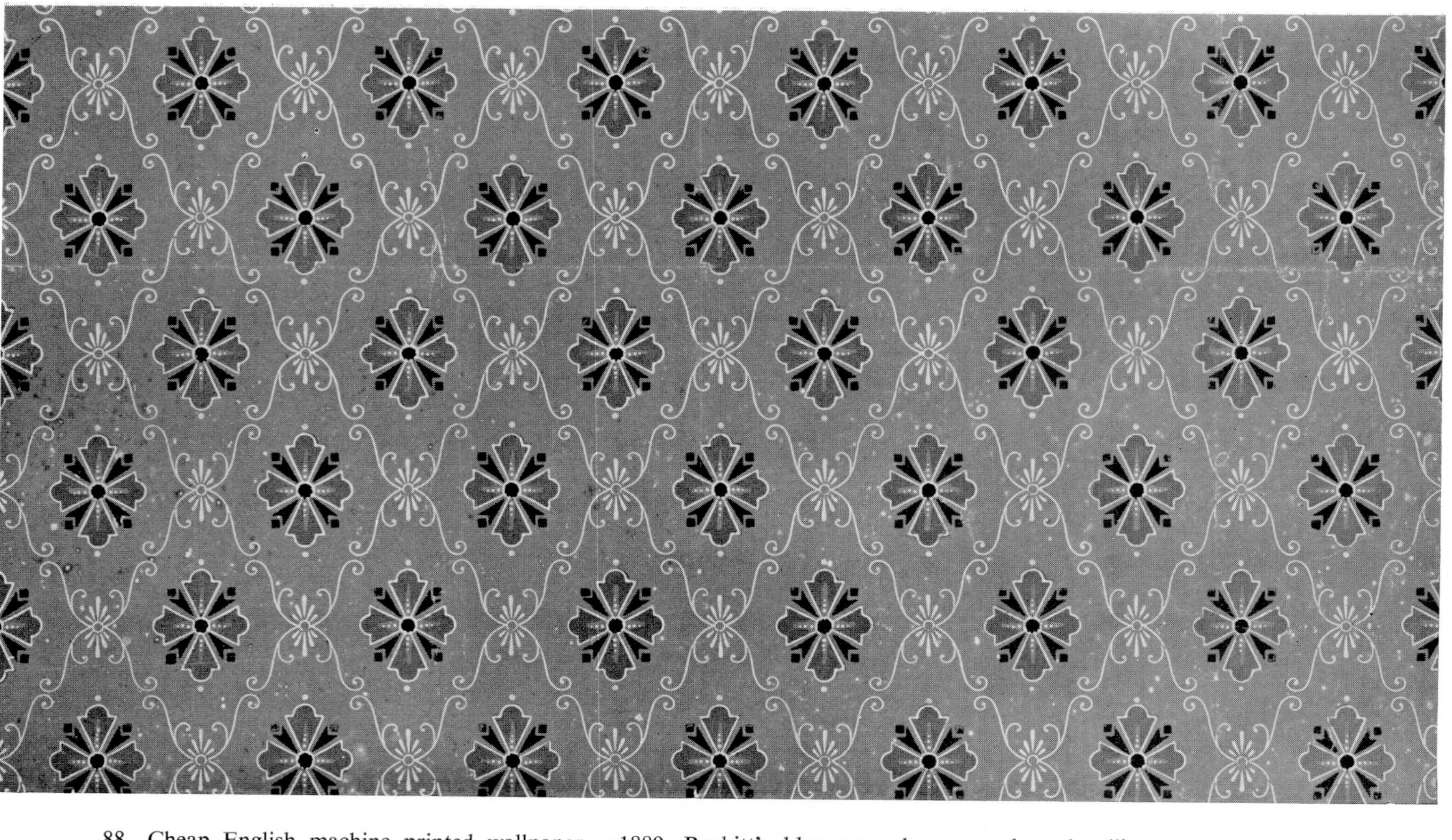

88 Cheap English machine printed wallpaper, *c*.1880. Reckitt's blue ground, cream-coloured trellis, maroon ornament

c. 1880 R. H. MOTTRAM, *The Window Seat* (1954). Referring to the 1880's:

. . . and latterly, when Mother turned our drawing room all William Morris the heavily patterned wallpaper was partly hidden by mezzotint reproductions of Leighton & the Pre-Raphaelites.

1880-81 GUY DE MAUPASSANT'S Short Story *Madame Tellier's Establishment.*

. . . The 'Jupiter' drawing room, where the local tradesmen foregathered, had a blue wallpaper adorned with a bold design of Leda reclining with the Swan.

[See also *Bel Ami* below.]

1881 *Decoration and Furniture of Town Houses,* SIR ROBERT. W. EDIS. Illustrated. General references.

1881 CLARENCE CHATHAM COOK, *What shall we do with our Walls?* Reference to Tapestry and probably to Wallpaper also. (Copy in Congress Library, U.S.A., not in B.M., London.)

1881 MRS. MARY E HAWEIS, *The Art of Decoration* (London), and other books on the same subject.

Of papers, those which emulate tapestry in a certain harmonious tone of broken colour are best. Many of Morris's papers copied from old 18th century ones, themselves copied from damask and leather patterns are very good. The well known grey pomegranate is really very fine indeed. A certain dark-red poppy pattern, wherein the flowers mingle dimly with a little gold, like sun rays in water (procurable at Elliotts, Vere Street), has a very good effect and throws up pictures and china well. . . etc.

Mrs. Haweis wrote a number of articles on interior decoration for the 'Ladies' Realm' about 1900 period.

1881 W. MATTIEU WILLIAMS, Arsenical Wallpapers. 'Science Notes', in *Gentleman's Magazine* (April). Ridicules the so-called dangers to health.

1881 YOUNG, *Every Man his own Mechanic.*

. . . Papers for sitting rooms may be procured at all prices from 1/– satins, ranging from 3/– to 6/–, and flocks being even more expensive.

1881 SPON'S *Encyclopaedia of Industrial Art* (London).

Imports of Paperhangings in 1879 were Sweden 7059 cwts=£8,351; France 5.583 cwts=£4,404. Others 880 cwts=£2,756.

1881 *The Journal of Decorative Art* (now *Painting and Decorating*) was first published this year: it has consistently served the interests of the Painting and Decorating trade in Great Britain since its inception, and has published many authoritative articles on wallpaper. It deserves study by all students of interior decoration. [See references below.]

1881 GUY DE MAUPASSANT, *Bel-Ami,* Chapter III.

The wallpaper, grey, with blue posies had as many stains as flowers, stains ancient and suspicious which defied analysis, crushed remains of insects, drops of oil, smudges of fingers greasy with pomade, splashes of soapsuds from the wash hand basin.

1882 THEODOR SEEMAN, *Die Tapete* (Vienna). Useful book historically.

1882 'Union Centrale des Arts Décoratifs.' 7° Exposition (*Le Papier Peint*, par V. PORTALET et P. RIOUX DE MAILBOU). Paris. Illustrated.

1882 WILLIAM MORRIS, *History of Pattern Designing*. One of the lectures given in support of the Society for the Protection of Ancient Buildings, the other being *The Lesser Arts of Life*. See below.

1882 WILLIAM MORRIS, *The Lesser Arts of Life*. A Lecture given in support of the Society for the Protection of Ancient Buildings. Part of a series in which R. S. Poole, Prof. W. B. Richmond, J. T. Micklethwaite, E. J. Poynter, R.A., and Wm. Morris participated. (Macmillan & Co., 1882).

I think the real way to deal successfully with designing for paperhangings is to accept their mechanical nature frankly, to avoid falling into the trap of trying to make your paper look as if it were painted by hand. Here is the place, if anywhere, for dots and lines and hatchings; mechanical enrichment is of the first necessity in it. . . . Some beautiful piece of nature must have pressed itself on our notice so forcibly that we are quite full of it and can, by submitting ourselves to the rules of art, express our pleasure to others . . .

A. V. SUGDEN, in his *History of English Wallpaper* (1926), quotes the following as being part of the above lecture, but this is not confirmed.

Whatever you have in your rooms, think first of the walls for they are that which make your house and home, and if you do not make some sacrifices in their favour you will find your chambers have a kind of make-shift, lodging-house look about them, however rich and handsome your moveables may be.

1883 Lecture. *Poisonous and Non-Poisonous Wall Colours and Wallpapers*. Read by STEVENSON MACADAM, Ph.D., Royal Scottish Society of Arts, Session 1881–2.

1883 PAINTED CLOTHS. GASTON LE BRETON, *Gazette des Beaux Arts*, 2e.S. XXVII, p. 170. 'Les Anciennes Toiles Peints et Imprimées a l'Exposition de l'Union Centrale.' [See also *Painted Wall Cloths in Sweden*, MRS. FRANCES MURRAY, also Depître].

1883 *The Art Journal*. 'Household Decoration—Wall Papers', G. T. ROBINSON.

The walls of too few of our houses are true enough to bear the test of mathematical division, hence flowing lines are more suitable. It is this objection which has led to the abandonment of the geometrically designed paperhangings which were so popular not long ago, and the general tendency of the design today is towards the more flowing and 'damasked' character of the seventeenth and eighteenth centuries.

Also: *It is very desirable that some technical museum should be established in which the best examples of the wallpapers produced each year should be preserved. Very much good decorative art is lost for the want of such a storehouse of design as the blocks rarely last more than a few years.*

1883 *Harper's Magazine* (February), 365/1.

The room remains in its original state, with the exception of the papering.

1884 G. ALLEN. *Philistia*, 1, 164.

I've had my room papered again since you saw it last.

89 A notable design by B. J. Talbert. The 'Sunflower': a machine printed wallpaper of 1878. (Victoria and Albert Museum)

90 Lewis F. Day. 'Apple Blossom': a wallpaper designed by this artist, *c*.1880. (*See* his numerous books on the subject of design and drawing.) (Victoria and Albert Museum)

1884 *Encyclopaedia Britannica* (9th edn.). Excellent article on wallpaper by WILLIAM MORRIS and J. H. MIDDLETON.

1885 EMILE ZOLA, *Germinal*, first published this year.

His wife (Mme Hennebeau) was explaining that she had not done anything about the office, which still had its old faded red wallpaper, heavy mahogany furniture and worn out card-board files.

1885 G. C. HAITÉ, *Wallpapers and their Manufacture*. A Lecture to The Society for the Encouragement of the Fine Arts (February 12). Reported in *The Building News* (February 20).

Mr. Haité remarked that the history of the manufacture for the last 50 years is built upon the efforts of such gifted men as the late Owen Jones, Welby Pugin, and Bruce Talbert, and of William Morris, Lewis Day, E. W. Godwin, Owen Davis, Walter Crane and others of the present day. The names of these designers are, he continued, as equally interwoven with the industry of wallpaper manufacture as are those of the great Eckhardt Bros, and Sherringham, and owing to the efforts of Mr. Scott (the oldest representative of the trade), Messrs. Warner, Aumonier and Game, the manufacture of today has been brought to the highest degree of excellence.

1886 F. FOLLOT, *Causerie sur le papier peint* (Paris). Illustrated.

1887 E. MAGLIN, *La Grande Encyclopédie* (Paris). 'Papiers Peints'.

En 1746, une première fabrique fut établie en Angleterre. Mais la fabrication n'y prit de l'extension qu'en 1870 avec Georges et Frederic Echardt on employait des planches gravées fort légères impregnées de couleur aux endroits utiles qu'on reportait sur le papier avec une impression suffisante. En France ce ne fut qu'a la fin du XVIIIe siècle que l'industrie prit naissance. En 1838 Bissonet inventa la première machine à imprimer en plusieurs couleurs. L'Anglais, Potter, inventa une machine à imprimer analogue à celle servant à l'impression des indiennes en toiles teintes. On multiplia le nombre des couleurs jusqu'on employa 54 tons différents à l'aide de la même machine. Mais le point de départ des machines à imprimer en plusieurs couleurs fut la machine de Bissonet.

1888 Arts and Crafts Exhibition Society started.

1889 FISHBACH, *Beitrag zur Geschichte der Tapeten Industrie* (Darmstadt).

1889 *Grand Dictionnaire Universel du XIXe siècle*, by M. PIERRE LAROUSSE. Contains an interesting contribution under 'Papiers Peints'.

1889 *The Art Journal* under 'Mural Decoration' (refers mainly to wallpaper makers, William Woollams Ltd. London).

In chronicling the advances which are taking place in Industrial Art there is no branch of which more note must be taken than that of Mural Decoration. Here the improvement is visible all along the line. It is hardly requisite for one to have been present at the stripping of a room where the old practice, now happily almost extinct, of pasting one wallpaper over another, has been in vogue, to be cognisant of the enormous chasm from the art point of view which separates the fabrics of today from those of say, the Great Exhibition year of 1851. It is seldom now that one encounters the gaudily gilt monstrosities (fitting prey for deleterious gassy fumes which quickly tarnished their lustre), or the heavily loaded 'flocks' shedding everywhere their poisonous dust. How all this is changed the Arts and Crafts Exhibition, where considerable space was devoted to wall-papers, testified.

1889 J. G. SHAW, *History and Traditions of Darwen and its People* (Toulmin, Printers, *The Times* Office, London). Pp. 160–1, 'Papermaking and Paperstaining'.

1889 International Exhibition. *Artisan Report.* J. T. SAMPSON, appointed delegate and practical paperstainer states:

The English style of design in the present day is, to my way of thinking, much in advance of the French.

1890 *The Darwen News* (July 2). The Jubilee Year of Belgrave Works, Darwen. Account of the history and development of Messrs. C. & J. G. Potter.

1890 LEWIS F. DAY, *Ornamental Design* (Batsford), Illustrated.

c. 1890 W. MACQUEEN-POPE, *Back Numbers* (Hutchinson, 1954). Refers to wall-papers of this period.

Extracts: p. 164. *The kitchen walls were covered with some kind of grained and varnished paper and its floor was covered with oil-cloth, but there was a rag mat before the fire, thick and heavy.* P. 181. (The Break-fast Room.) *The carpet was Brussells and the walls covered with a grey paper bearing bunches of red flowers, but time had toned down the red and the effect was quite pleasing.* P. 199. The Drawing Room *was black and gold or perhaps yellow and black. The wallpaper was yellow with vertical stripes, shiny and matt, the shiny somehow seeming the lightest. Thus a satin-like effect was attained.* P. 213. (The Hall.) *It had a Turkey carpet in it and several rugs and the wallpaper was a mottled brown, with a broad dado.* P. 218. (The Front Bedroom.) *It had a thick Turkey carpet on the floor and a light wallpaper—white, with immense flowers on it, species quite unknown, but partaking of the nature of a dahlia, a chrysanthemum, a rose and a cabbage all at the same time, and of a bright blue tint. There was a wardrobe of mahogany large enough to live in, etc.*

[See 1954.]

1891 W. R. BRADSHAW, *Wallpaper, Its History, Manufacture and Decorative Importance* (New York). (Copy in Library of Congress, U.S.A.)

1891 VYVYAN HOLLAND, *Son of Oscar Wilde* (Hart-Davis, 1954.) Reference to Oscar Wilde's smoking room at Tite Street, Chelsea, about this period.

The walls were covered with the peculiar wallpaper of that period, known as Lincrusta Walton, and had a William Morris pattern of dark red and dull gold. When you poked it with your finger, it popped and split, and your finger might even go through, so this was not much encouraged. The décor was North African. Divans, Ottomans, Moorish hangings, and lan-terns filled the room. Glass bead curtains hung before the windows. . . .

On p. 56 there is a description of Lady Mount Temple's house, Babba-combe Cliff, designed by Ruskin and decorated largely by William Morris and Burne Jones.

All the other rooms in the house bore the names of flowers according to the pattern of their wallpaper; Daisy, Lily, Primrose, Poppy, Marigold and so on. . . .

1891 W. SCOTT MORTON, R.S.S.A., *Tynecastle Embossed Canvas.* Read before The Royal Scottish Society of Arts (November 23). Apropos Leather Hangings.

But in a period of artistic laxity, when an effective and costly decoration becomes fashionable, there is a temptation to imitate it in a cheap and showy fabric, and we find that in France and England printed papers were introduced in imitation of leathers.

1892 From *Works Rules* at a London wallpaper factory dated September 1.

Anyone who in the aggregate, is over 30 minutes late during the week will be fined as follows:

Those earning up to 10/–	*2d.*
Exceeding 10/– and not exceeding 15/–	*3d.*
,, *15/–* ,, ,, ,, *20/–*	*4d.*
,, *20/–*	*6d.*

If over 60 and under 120 minutes late double the above.
If over 180 minutes late time to be stopped in addition to the above double fines.

N.B. This rule will be strictly enforced irrespective of Rank or Class.

1892 JAMES POPE-HENNESSY, *Memoirs of Queen Mary* (Allen and Unwin, 1959).

In December 1892 Prince George had been over York Cottage several times with 'Maple's man' and assisted by his father, the Prince of Wales and by his eldest sister Princess Louise, Duchess of Fife, he had chosen patterns for all carpets and wallpapers.

1893 J. S. CORDER, *Christchurch, or Withepole House, Ipswich.* Reference to flock wallpapers.

1893 T. R. SPENCE, *Wallpapers and Stencilling.* Paper read before The Royal Society of Arts (February 21). Illustrated by line drawings of designs by Walter Crane, Lewis F. Day, L. Aumonier, T. W. Hay, C. F. A. Voysey, T. R. Spence, etc.

Two of the most important qualities in decorative design for wallpapers, should, I take it, be a general flatness and colour harmony.

1893 JOHN KAY, *Paper, Its History* (Smith Kay & Co. London). Contains on p. 74 some notes on the history of wallpaper based on T. R. Spence's paper above.

1894 *The Studio* (December). 'A Designer of Paperhangings.' Interview with Walter Crane.

It was in 1874 that Mr. Metford Warner the principal of Messrs. Jeffrey & Co. invited me to prepare a cartoon for a nursery paper as far as might be in the manner of my illustrated toy-books, a certain number of which, as you are aware, had then already appeared. This first paper comprised three groups of pictures illustrative of popular nursery-rhymes, 'Little

Boy Blue', 'Sing a Song of Sixpence', etc. It was issued in 1875 and was succeeded by the 'Humpty Dumpty' paper in 1876. . . . etc.

1895 CHARLES BOOTH, *Life and Labour of the People in London.* This great sociological work contains valuable notes on Block and Machine printing, Flocking, Embossing, Wages, Methods of Learning, Hours, Seasons, Health, etc. See under 'Industry', Vol. 2.

In London the Trade is decreasing, the number of persons returned as paper-stainers falling from 1,101 in 1881, to 1,031 in 1891; these numbers include the dealers, and as there is no reason to suppose their *numbers have declined . . . the proportionate reduction of the number of workmen is probably greater than shown above. The decrease seems to lie with the block-printers, machine work taking the place of the block-printed papers.*

1895 JEAN ZUBER, *Réminiscences et Souvenirs de Jean Zuber père* (Mulhouse).

1895 C. F. A. VOYSEY, *The Aims and Conditions of the Modern Decorator* (February 15). Paper read in Manchester to the Association of Master Plasterers and Painters. Reported in full in *Journal of Decorative Art*, April, 1895.

1895 SHIRLEY HIBBERD, *Rustic Adornments for Homes of Taste.* Illustrations of variegated ivies with instructions for their use in decorative schemes.

1895 FREDERIC AUMONIER, *Wallpapers, their Manufacture and Design.* A paper read before the Society of Architects.

1895 LEWIS F. DAY, *Good Words*, (April) p. 244. 'The Art and Craft of Paper-staining.'

1896 METFORD WARNER, *History of Paperhangings.* Read before The Art Workers' Guild.

I do not propose to continue my notes beyond the Paris Exhibition of 1878, but there has since been marked improvement in the designs and production of machine printed papers while the artistic value and quality of those printed by hand or blocks has been fully maintained and I am glad to think that such wallpapers are no longer treated as 'mere makeshift' but that they take their own place as a definite material for the use of beautifying our homes.

1897 AYMER (WILLIAM HOWARD) VALLANCE. *The Art of William Morris* with reproductions from designs and fabrics printed in the colours of the originals (Bell and Sons, London).

1897 From an article 'A Christmas of the Past', *Cabinet Makers and Complete House Furnisher*, December 20, 1947. Relating to the 1890's:

At many festive gatherings the proud lady of the house was able to call attention to the artistic wallpaper with which her rooms were decorated. For, as with furniture, the year had witnessed big strides in the development of this article. At an Exhibition at Earl's Court, an outstanding feature had been a display of wallpapers from 1837–1897 by the London firm William Woollams Ltd. This had aroused widespread interest and focused attention on the need for better taste in the wall decorations of the home. The display emphasized that the gaudy colours and florid designs of a previous generation had given way to quieter and more subdued motifs . . .

91 Wallpaper border in the foyer of the recently restored Vienna Opera House. This was printed by Weiner Tapetenfabrik A.G. of Vienna, suppliers of the original wallpaper. The white space shown on the left of the illustration has still to be filled

92 Wallpaper design drawn by William Morris for Balmoral Castle, 1887. The pencilled note states 'Their majesties prefer this design with the diamonds as big again . . . the design to be in flock (not coloured)'

1897 JEAN ZUBER ET CIE. *La fabrique de papiers peints de Jean Zuber à Rixheim 1797–1897.*

1897 ROSAMUND MARRIOTT WATSON, *Art of the House*, pp. 185, (Geo. Bell & Sons Ltd). Illustrated. An unusually strong condemnation of many of the wallpapers of this period occurs in the first chapter of this book.

Extracts . . . *The 'Art' wallpaper with its misbegotten sun flowers and poppies, its inane sham mediaeval dicky birds intermixed with geometrical patternings, its livid complexion, now sour now sallow, but ever revolting, they are all in the same tale. To be sure they have mainly ebbed out to the suburbs but that is only so much worse for the suburbs.*

Elsewhere: *That school of mural decoration for which the designs of Mr. William Morris may be taken as the leading type falls, despite its obvious, (sometimes a little too obvious) virtues, into the common error of considering wallpaper as an independent system of decoration in itself as a portion of the general scheme . . . a background for the contents of the chamber whose nakedness it is to cover, etc.*

(The author is eventually convinced, though not all her readers surely, that wallpaper is 'out' and that only wood panelling, old tapestry and old Spanish or Italian leather are fit wall coverings for the home of good taste. The book is based on articles which appeared in the *Pall Mall Gazette* under the heading 'Wares of Autolycus').

1898 STUART W. PROVERBS, *Design for Wallpapers.* A paper read to The Society of Designers, and reported in two consecutive numbers of *The Artist* with illustrations. '. . .*Of course there are many processes in wallpaper making which are more or less in the nature of trade secrets, but those I have described will give you some idea of the intense interest inseparable from the manufacture of and designing for wallpaper.*'

1898 AYMER VALLANCE, *The Art Journal*, 'Wallpaper Design and Manufacture'.

1898 *The Artist* (September–December). Seventeenth-century wallpapers described by LINDSAY P. BUTTERFIELD.

1898 *The Child's Guide to Knowledge*. Simkin Marshall & Co.

Cheap papers are now printed by means of a revolving cylinder which produces all the colours at once. Q: How many yards will one of these machines print in a day? A: Upwards of 18,000 and the pattern is printed on the paper in lengths of half a mile; Q: Are they not then divided? A: Yes, into lengths of twelve yards.

1898 WALL PAPER MERCHANTS' ASSOCIATION. Inaugural Meeting July 20 in Manchester.

1898 From an American wallpaper dealers' advertisement:

Make selections at your home from the famous Alfred Peat's 1898 Art Wallpapers. Over 500 new patterns to show you in my sample books which are the same papers as will be sold at Alfred Peat & Co's mammoth New York and Chicago stores this year. New floral, silk, cretonne, chintz, Delft, denim and stripe effects for Parlors and Bedrooms at 3c. to 10c. per roll. Beautiful and High Class tapestry, damask, colonial, embossed leather, Louis XIV, Empire, Byzantine, Moorish, Rococo, Marie Antoinette stripes. Rich floral and satin effects . . . etc.

1899 *The Art Journal* (March), 'Recent Industrial Art' by 'E.F.V.' Illustrated.

The difficulty of choosing wallpapers is one which has been felt by all those lucky or unlucky enough to have had at any period to face the ordeal of furnishing a house. The variety of styles, colours and designs still further tend to bewilder the chooser, but happily there are certain houses where a bad choice is impossible.

(Then follows comment on new wallpapers by Jeffrey & Co., Essex & Co., Rottmann & Co., Knowles & Co.)

1899 J. W. MACKAIL, *The Life of William Morris* (Longmans & Co., London), p. 156. Reference to Morris's use of etched plates at this date.

1899 *Practical Designing*, edited by GLEESON WHITE (Geo. Bell & Sons, London). Illustrated. Chapter on Wallpaper designing by GEO. C. HAITÉ, R.B.A.

The charm of repetition lies most frequently in its simplicity. It must also be borne in mind that the more severe the treatment of design the better it will bear repetition: the closer it follows or verges upon the naturalesque the less satisfactory it becomes the oftener it is repeated.

1899 LEWIS F. DAY, *Easter Annual Advertiser*, 'William Morris and his Art'.

1900 PAUL LAFOND, *L'Art décoratif et le mobilier sous la République, etc.* 'Le papier', p. 213. Illustrated, Paris.

1900 AUGUSTIN BLANCHET, *Essai sur l'histoire du papier, etc.* (B.M. copy destroyed).

1900 REV. H. E. RADBOURNE, *Henry Lightbown*, Life of the founder of the Lightbown Aspinall wallpaper mill, originally in Manchester, now at Bredbury, nr. Stockport.

1900 FOLLOT, *Rapport du Comité d'Installation de la Classe 68*. Papiers peints à l'Exposition Universelle (Paris).

1900 From SIR JOHN SQUIRE's review of JOHN MASEFIELD's autobiography *So Long to Learn* in *Illustrated London News* (April 5, 1952). Reference to Yeat's Monday evenings in Woburn Buildings fifty years ago.

For me alas, all I can remember is that the room was hung with brown paper and lit with candles, and that the atmosphere was rather hieratic.

1900 Oscar Wilde. Reputed last words in the Hotel d'Alsace, Paris: 'My wallpaper is killing me, one of us must go.' LADY GREGORY'S MEMOIRS.

1900 COMPTON MACKENZIE, *Sinister Street*, Book Three, Chapter IV (reference to 1900 period).

There was his mother's own sitting room whose rose du Barri cushions and curtains conformed exactly to his own preconceptions, and there was Stella's bedroom very white and severe, and his own bedroom pleasantly mediaeval, and the dining room very cool and green, and the drawing room with wallpaper of brilliant Chinese birds and in a brass cage a blue and crimson macaw blinking at the sombre Thames.

93 English machine printed wallpaper designed from drawings by Kate Greenaway, *c.*1893

94 The 'Compton' wallpaper, designed by William Morris, 1895. (Victoria and Albert Museum)

95 The 'Knapweed' design by Heywood Sumner for Jeffrey & Co., Islington, in 1900. (Victoria and Albert Museum)

96 Characteristic of the *fin de siècle* style. A frieze designed, and blocks cut, by William Shand Kydd in 1896

1900 A. E. V. LILLEY and W. MIDGELEY, *A Book of Studies in Plant form with some suggestions for their Application to Design.* Illustrated. (Chapman & Hall). [See Chapter on 'Wallpaper' with some fine floral studies in black and white].

1900 BRUEHLER, *Die Tapete und Elsass* (Das Kunstgewebe in Elsass—Lothringen, Strasburg).

1900 IVOR BROWN in his memoirs *The Way of my World* (Collins, 1954) mentions C. P. Scott's Manchester House at this period,

. . . a house furnished in late Victorian taste, with Morris wallpapers and an air of serenity.

C. P. Scott was the famous editor of *The Manchester Guardian.*

1900 MARCEL PROUST, in *Remembrance of Things Past,* 'A la Recherche du Temps Perdu.' (Reference to the first decade of twentieth century.)

The walls of my dressing room were covered with a paper on which a violent red background was patterned with black and white flowers to which it seemed that I should have some difficulty in growing accustomed. But they succeeded only as striking me as novel, in forcing me to enter not into conflict with them, but into contact with them in modulating the gaiety, the songs of my morning toilet. They succeeded only in imprisoning me in the heart of a sort of poppy, out of which to look at a world quite different from in Paris.

1900 *The Book of the Home.* Edited by H. C. Davidson. 8 Vols. Illustrated. Chapter on Wall Coverings, Vol. 1, p. 73, probably written by MRS. HAWEIS [See 1881].

. . . the artistic quality of wallpapers is not however always in exact proportion to the price, as some of the expensive papers are very ugly and some of the cheap ones excellent in design.

Under the heading 'Professional and Amateur Decorating Compared' this book deals with the art of paperhanging in detail for the benefit of the amateur. 'Painting and papering an ordinary room in an ordinary way', it states, 'is not a very formidable undertaking' and then shows that about half the cost of decorating can be saved by doing it yourself!

Elsewhere: '*Bedroom papers.*' *The design of a bedroom paper is important. It must not be 'spotty', it must not repeat itself too frequently or 'run into lines' and it must not be one of those eccentric and irritating patterns of flying birds that 'never get any forrader' or of cherubs sitting insecurely on prickly roses, or chasing butterflies that they never catch. Even the designs of bows and ribbons and high handled baskets of flowers falling over the sides, which have been popular of late, are apt, pretty enough in themselves though they may be, to grow annoying when they have to be contemplated during the long feverish hours of an invalid's day. Whether floral patterned papers are altogether desirable in bedrooms is a moot point. They are often very graceful and charming, but the majority have a tendency to fidgetiness, which is strengthened when the curtains match the paper in pattern as some decorative authorities advise. . . . The best type of paper is one which has a purely conventional pattern of natural foliage in two shades of one colour. There may be a frieze, either of plain colour wash or ingrain paper, or, if a stronger relief is required, of festoons of flowers. Striped papers in two tones of colour look particularly well under a wide floral frieze.* [Continued overleaf].

The so-called washable papers are perfect from a sanitary point of view for bedroom walls, but as a matter of fact they will bear nothing more than the most cautious and gentle sponging. . . .

c. 1900 REBECCA WEST, *The Fountain Overflows.* (Referring to early 20th century.)

I was incensed for another reason by the straw wallpaper so faintly striped by a designer who used gold without ostentation, without thought for its secondary value as a sign of wealth, simply for its beauty. Lately the rain had got into Mamma's room through a faulty gutter, and Mamma had had to have it redecorated with the plainest paper because it was the cheapest.

1901 FELIX FOLLOT, *Musée retrospectif de la classe 68 a l'Exposition de 1900 à Paris.* Papiers peints. (St. Cloud, gr in 8°, fig. et pl.)

1901 HORACE WARNER, *Art Journal.* 'How Wallpapers are Printed' (by a Practical Paperstainer). Illustrated. Refers solely to hand printing processes.

1901 *Commerce* (April 10), Vol. XVI, No. 406. Illustrated weekly journal. Contains description of Sandersons, Chiswick and Berners Street.

. . . a very few years ago the cry of cheapness was so persistent in the trade that the manufacturers literally began to despair for the future of their high class goods. That cheap wave passed. The people have now learned to recognize the value of a good thing, and especially have they done so since the introduction of electric lighting superseded the surface destroying glare and fumes of murky gas.

Elsewhere in this article: . . . *one of the showrooms* (*at Sandersons*), *is now being fitted to display the designs of the firm of Wm. Woollams & Co. who have recently closed their premises. Mr. Webbe, a partner in the late firm, has joined Sandersons and the wonderful designs by past masters of the art, such as Owen Jones, will shortly appear in new colourings.*

And: . . . *the pendulum swings, and the old world chintzes, despised by the 'greenery-yallery' school of the seventies, now appear again on the walls of the best houses . . .*

1902 P. G. KONODY, *The Art of Walter Crane* (Bell, London).

1902 AYMER VALLANCE, *Art Journal,* 'New Designs for Wallpaper'.

1903 *Home Arts and Crafts.* Edited and compiled by MONTAGUE MARKS. (C. Arthur Pearson Ltd., London.) An early manifestation of the 'Do-it-Yourself' craze including instructions for Poker Work, Etching, Bent-iron work, Fret-sawing, Taxidermy and Wallpaper Designing.

Manufacturers, as a rule, prefer simple patterns conventionally treated to floral and other patterns needing many printings. The more colours, or shades of the same colour, *that are called for in a design, the more printings are required to reproduce that design, and hence, as a rule, the smaller the chance of its acceptance by the manufacturer. In estimating the number of printings required, each shade has to be reckoned as a separate colour, because it calls for a separate printing. A single printing will only give a perfectly flat impression*—i.e., *uniform in light and shade. The only possible modification of this uniformity is by means of stippling, which breaks the tones of the parts so treated. This device is seldom re-*

sorted to except in the case of very cheap wall-papers, and need not be taken into account by the novice in designing.

Avoid the use of pronounced figures and any arrangement that tends to produce the effect of horizontal lines, and remember that although a pattern may be pleasing on a small piece of paper, it may weary the eye and lose character when spread over a large surface like that of a wall.

'Dimensions of a Design'—Almost invariably the dimensions of a design for an English wall-paper are 21 in. × 21 in., the paper itself being 22 in., the extra inch allowing a margin on each side for the register of the block in printing, and also as a protection to the edges of the roll. The space, 21 in. × 21 in., may be divided into squares of five different dimensions as follows: First, four squares of 10½ in. × 10½ in.; second, nine squares of 7 in.; third, sixteen squares of 5¼ in.; fourth, twenty-five squares of 4⅕ in.; fifth, forty-nine squares of 3 in.* Mr. George C. Haité, in his admirably lucid paper on Wall-Papers, in 'Practical Designing' [see 1899], *which no student of the subject can afford to miss, points out that these five divisions of the space 'would limit the fancy and play of the designer, were it not possible to get over the difficulty by a still further division of the width by means of what is called* stepping *the design—a method which is most valuable and of frequent use; for it is not only that by this means a different* scale *of work is possible, but that by its adoption we are enabled to better disguise the 'repeat' and to render the effect of a mass of 'repeats' covering a large surface more satisfactory and pleasant in line.'*

'The Repeat'—The principles of the 'repeat' and the application of the device of 'stepping' are set forth clearly by Mr. Haité. A pattern, he says, 'should either boldy declare its repeat, and indeed make a feature of it, or it should not be noticeable at all; and, further, all repeats should be pleasant to the eye, avoiding disagreeable lines, some of which may even make the wall appear out of the upright or undulating. Unless intentional, as a feature of the pattern, it is well to disguise all *lines. The perpendicular is less objectional than the horizontal, and the true diagonal line less so than either.'*

1902 *The Decorator* (London). A monthly journal devoted to the interests of the decorating trade established this year. Also publishes a Year Book giving up-to-date information concerning wallpaper manufacturers and dealers in this country. [See references below].

1903 *The Craftsman.* Illustrations of Wallpaper Design.

1903.. GEORGE GISSING, *The Private Papers of Henry Ryecroft*, Chapter 1.
. . . as to such trifles as the tint and device of wallpaper I confess my indifference; be the walls only unobtrusive and I am satisfied.

1903 A. S. JENNINGS,† *Wallpapers and Wall Coverings* (London). [This book contains a wealth of information relating to wallpaper at this period and, fortunately, the book although published nearly 60 years ago is not difficult to come by. It contains many illustrations and also advertisements of English and American wallpaper makers of the day]. (*see over*).

* The *Register* indicates on the paper the limits of a certain colour, upon which the successive printings of the other colours of the design must not impinge. The adjustment of the register in all colour printing must be extremely accurate.

† One time Editor of 'The Decorator' Magazine. He died in 1928.

Wallpaper Fashions in 1903. It rarely happens in the wallpaper trade that a season brings any marked change in fashions or in the public taste. One season will see perhaps the advent of a new style or new colouring and this gradually develops and grows stronger until it reaches its zenith when it may hold for some years and then decline. Speaking generally those styles which come quickly into favour do not last long in popularity. In 1903 there is a distinct demand for pearls and grays and a beginning of a demand for panel decoration and the old fashioned moirés. Striped papers continue to be very popular while ingrains are stronger than ever, especially those having spotted or diaper designs very feebly printed. Landscape friezes are certainly much in demand and some very useful works are now to be obtained, the landscape being by hand in such a manner that the parts may be changed so as to accommodate the space to be filled in decorating a room. . . . One of the most encouraging signs of the times is the demand for papers of simple design without that excessive elaboration which is so unsatisfactory because it kills the repose necessary in the sitting room. At the same time in halls and large staircases, where considerable expanse of wall space is to be covered, and where there is little or no furniture, exceedingly bold and bright coloured designs continue to be popular.

c. 1904 RICHARD CHURCH, *Over the Bridge* (Heinemann, 1953). Reference to his parents' Dulwich House.

The little drawing room was lined with lincrusta, of a bold, oriental splendour in gold. [See 1907 below].

1904 EDITH WHARTON and OGDEN CODMAN, *The Decoration of Houses*, (Batsford).

It was well for the future of house decoration when medical science declared itself against the use of wallpapers. These hangings have little to recommend them. Besides being objectionable on sanitary grounds, they are inferior as a wall decoration to any form of treatment, however simple, that maintains, instead of effacing, the architectural lines of a room.

1904 *Haydyn's Dictionary of Dates*, 23rd Edition. '*Paperhangings. Stamped paper for this purpose was first made in Spain and Holland about 1555: made of velvet and floss for hanging apartments in 1620.*' Also entries under 'Papier Maché', etc.

1904 *Life and Letters of M. Creighton*, Chapter 1, 83.

He is spoken of as being the first to introduce the inhabitants of Falmouth to Morris's wallpapers.

1904 LEWIS F. DAY, *Ornament and its Application* (Batsford). Illustrated.

Equally bad offenders at present are the French who seem to have no other idea of a wallpaper than to make it look like damask, lace, embroidery, mosaic, painting, tapestry, no matter what, so long as it has no character of printed paper.

1904 AYMER VALLANCE, *Magazine of Art*, 'Wallpapers'.

1905 KATE SANBORN, *Old Time Wallpapers* (New York). A useful source book, but in a friendly, gossipy way. (*Continued on page 145*)

Plate 1 in her book is not eighteenth century but nineteenth. Plate 2 is certainly not 100 years old.

97 Typical of many English machine printed wallpaper chintz designs at the turn of the century

98 A nursery wallpaper designed by Jessie M. King about 1906–10. (Victoria and Albert Museum)

For although a native of New Hampshire. I was born at the foot of Mount Vesuvius and there was a merry dance to the music of mandolin and tambourine round the tomb of Vergil on my natal morn. Some men are fishing, others bringing in the catch; farther on was a picnic party, sentimental youths and maidens eating comfits and dainties, to the tender notes of a flute, and old Vesuvius was smoking violently. All this because the room in which I made my débût was adorned with a landscape on scenic wallpaper.

1905 G. A. FOSTER, *Morley's Philatelic Journal* (November), 'Wallpaper Tax'.

1905 A. G. B. RUSSELL, *Burlington Magazine* (July). '17th Century wallpaper at Wotton-under-Edge' . The author has been proved at fault in classifying this English wallpaper as Chinese. [See 1909, etc.]

1905 *Journal of Decorative Art* (September.) Contains interesting review of the prominent mills and personalities of the English wallpaper industry at this date.

1905 H. G. WELLS, *Kipps*

. . . Revel came at last, politely admiring in a flute-like voice the mellow wallpaper of the stair-case.

1906 *Who's Who in Business*

Jeffrey & Co: 64 Essex Road, Islington. London N. West End Showrooms: The Wallpaper Gallery, 31, Mortimer Street, Regent St., W. Established forty years ago when the firm was inaugurated as the result of an amalgamation of Jeffrey & Co. and Holmes and Aubert. Mr. Metford Warner has directed the firm for thirty years; his sons, who were brought up in it, assist in the management. The first machines erected in London for printing wallpapers were erected at the Whitechapel factory (of Jeffrey & Co.), and ever since the firm have been printers of high class machine printed papers. Specialities: the highest class of hand printed wallpapers including all classes of flocks, and embossed leather papers. These have been produced from the designs of the leading decorative artists of the day, and their merit has been recognized at all the International Exhibitions. . . . The spacious galleries in Mortimer Street were opened in 1902

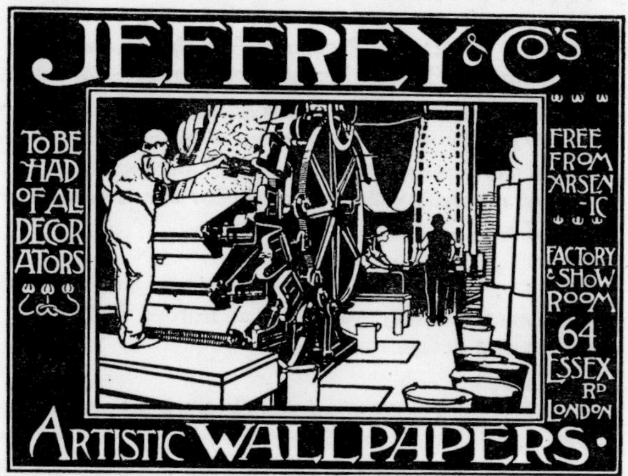

99 Delightfully drawn advertisement of Jeffrey & Co. Ltd., Islington

1906 *Journal of Decorative Art*, p. 323. 'Saltfleet Manor House Wallpaper.' Description of a very early flock wallpaper.

1907 J. J. BECKETT, *Paperhangings*. Delivered in Darwen (Lancs.), Library Lecture Hall (February 1). Copies of this lecture now unobtainable except in private collections, but this is an important and well thought-out account of the English wallpaper industry. Comments on Taxation and Manufacturing are particularly interesting.

1907 RICHARD CHURCH, in his Autobiography *Over the Bridge* (Chapter 10). Reference to his parents' Battersea house at this period:

> *Mother's revolt against thrift consisted first, of having the kitchen re-decorated in a wallpaper of gay open pattern that appeared to double the size of the room. For the first time 'art' entered our Victorian home, bringing light and gaiety.* (See above 1904).

1908 F. G. FROGGATT, *Studio Year Book of Decorative Art*, 'Wall and Ceiling Decoration'. The first of these annuals appeared in 1906.

1909 MARGARET JOURDAIN, *The Connoisseur* (August), 'Chinese Wallpapers in England'.

1909 *Journal of Decorative Art* (December). 'A Wallpaper Order given in 1737.'

1909 *Journal of Decorative Art*. 29., 447. 'Seventeenth-Century Wallpaper at Wotton-under-Edge.'

1909 Musée Galliéra, Paris. *Exposition des Papiers et Toiles Imprimés*. '*Catalogue of exhibits*', which included products of Ch. Follot; Defossé et Karth; Lincrusta Walton, etc.

1910 *Encyclopaedia Britannica*, 11th edn. Article by JAMES BARTLETT, lecturer on Architecture etc., Kings College London.

> *The term wallpaper embraces a very large variety of materials of many kinds, designs and qualities, ranging from the cheapest machine-printed papers of the most flimsy description, and often hideous design, to the Japanese and similar leather papers.*

1910 METFORD WARNER, *Progress of Design in Paperhangings*. Read before The Institute of British Decorators (January 10). London.

> *The London Annual Exhibition of All Fine Arts, Industries and Inventions in 1873, gave me the opportunity of claiming that paperhangings designed by such artists as I have mentioned,* were works of art, a claim which was at first resisted by the authorities but was eventually acceeded to, and the medal award was valued accordingly.*

1910 E. FOLEY, *Book of Decorative Furniture*, Vol. 1, p. 96. Reference to an old sixteenth-century wallpaper at Borden Hall, Kent. Includes remarks on taste and design trends.

ELSEWHERE:

> *It is becoming recognised that design is no occult, mysterious thing, but very tangible and sensible, capable of giving new interest to the commonest object of daily life. Who was it said so happily, that Design is not the off-*

* B. J. Talbert; E. W. Godwin; Owen Jones; Dr. Dresser, etc.

spring of idle fancy, but the studied result of accumulated observation and delightful habit? It is good to realise that merit of 'originality' is not novelty, nor the catching of customers; it is fitness and sincerity. To encourage the bud of originality, to break through the sheath of precedent is well, but in the modern studio the process is, perforce often more reminiscent of the hunting of the snark.

1910 FRANK H. VIZETELLY, *The New Age Magazine* (November), p. 389. 'Wallpapers, their Origin and History.'

1910 *Art Journal* (p. 91). Article on 'Wallpapers' illustrated with contemporary examples in half-tone.

1910 *Notes & Queries*, 11th Series, 1, p. 350. Reference to a painted paper at Bradbourne Hall, Derby (*c.* 1700).

1911 C. SAYLE, *The Library*, 3rd Series, II, p. 340. 'Cambridge Fragments.'

1911 E. J. DUVEEN, *Colour in the Home* (George Allen). Brief reference to obtrusive wallpapers.

1912 HENRI CLOUZOT, *Gazette des Beaux Arts*, Vol. VII, 'La Tradition du Papier Peint en France au XVIIe et XVIIIe siècles.'

1912 FERNAND ROCHE, *L'Art Décoratif* (February), 'Vieux Papiers Peints'.

1912 L. BOUTEILLE, *L'Art Décoratif* (September), 'Les Vieux Décors en Papier Peint'.

1912 ELSIE DE WOLFE, *The House in Good Taste* (New York). Typical of many books on interior decoration published at home and abroad at this time and since. This publication which ran to several editions is better than most, although containing unkind criticisms of wallpaper. '*If I could find perfect (smooth) walls,*' the author says at one point, '*I'd always paint them, and never use a yard of paper!*'

1912 WALTHER HALVORSEN, 'Old French Wallpapers in Norway', *Art and Culture*, 1912–13, 3, pp. 107–13.

1912 PAINTED CLOTHS. E. DEPÎTRE, *La Toile Peinte en France* (Paris). A protest against the current taxation of painted and printed linens, etc. Of passing interest owing to its historical references to painted cloths.

1912 J. and E. R. PENNELL, 'Whistler as Decorator', *Century Magazine*, Vol. 83, p. 506. New York.

1913 PAPER MAKING. J. GRAND-CARTERET, *Papeterie et Papetiers*, 340 pp., 160 illustrations (Paris). A very detailed history of various trades associated with paper, which includes an account of the Dominotiers, Imagiers et Tapissiers. The book seems to have been compiled during, or as a result of, the International Exhibition of 1900 in Paris.

1912-13 GUSTAV IVEN (a Hamburg wallpaper manufacturer). Very interesting article on the German industry contributed to *Tapeten Zeitung* (German Wallpaper Magazine) about this time.

1913 MARCEL PROUST, *A La Recherche du Temps Perdu* (Remembrance of Things Past), Swann's Way, Part II.

In place of the lovely gowns in which Mme Swann walked like a queen, appeared Greco-Roman tunics with Tanagra folds, or sometimes in the Directoire style, Liberty chiffons sprinkled with flowers like sheets of wallpaper.

1913 P. GUSMAN, *Panneaux Décoratifs et Tentures Murales du XVIIIe siècle.*

1913 NOEL D. SHEFFIELD. A Paper read to the Society of Architects March 13 and reported in *Journal of Society of Architects* (April), 'Wallpapers'. This is an amusingly provocative and discerning lecture containing some shrewd comments on the industry and wallpaper user. In a discussion following, C. F. A. Voysey and H. W. Sanderson both spoke at some length. Mr. Sheffield demonstrated that wallpaper was now being taken up by architects after they had given it up in despair because of its degradation of taste in design. He tilted at the Ladies' 'Fashion Papers' because of the injudicious advice they gave to amateur decorators, and blamed the small decorator who was often a sanitary engineer and plumber as well, for perpetuating bad taste in the selection of papers he offered his clients.

1913 PAUL SCHULZE, *Etwas über Supraporten und ältere Tapetendruck*, Vol. 6, p. 420.

1913 Austrian Museum for Art and Industry, Vienna. Catalogue of an Exhibition of Austrian Wallpaper, containing a good introduction to the subject by Dr. Edward Leisching, who was director of the above museum at this time.

1913-14 *Adresbuch der Tapeten* (*Wallpaper*)*—Linoleum—Linkrusta—Buntglaspapier* (*Diaphanic paper*) *Fabriken Aller Länder der Welt*. Ausgabe, 1913–14. M. Schulze. Alsleben. a S. A very comprehensive directory containing the addresses of most of the European makers of wallpaper at this date. Quite unique in this respect and most useful to the historian. The list of English makers is extremely well compiled.

1914 CLAUDE ROGER-MARX, *Bon Ton*, 'Du Choix d'un Papier Peint'.

Si nous voulons nous souvenir de telle époque de notre existence, lié aux moindres actions, nous revoyons le papier peint sur lequel rôdèrent nos yeux; notre pensée reste mêlee aux fleurs qui clairisement les murs et comme colorée par elles. Pierre Nozière, dans le Livre de mon Ami* *évoque le temps où sa mère lui fit don d'une rose de la tenture. L'orsqu'on nous conte les adolescences de Clara d'Ellé beuse ou d'Almaïde d'Etremont, aussitôt apparaît le papier à feuillages et à grands oiseaux romantiques qui tapissait leur alcove.*

*[By ANATOLE FRANCE. English version is: 'One day in the little drawing room, she put down her work and, picking me up in her arms, pointed to one of the flowers on the wall, saying, "I will give you this rose", and so that there might be no mistake, she made a cross on it with her bodkin. No present ever made me happier'].

1914 E. G. HESSLING, *Le Style Directoire étoffes et papiers de Tenture.*

1914 FRANCIS LENYGON, '*Decoration in England 1660–1770*'. (Batsford). Contains a short chapter on the history of wallpaper. Reference to Chinese papers:

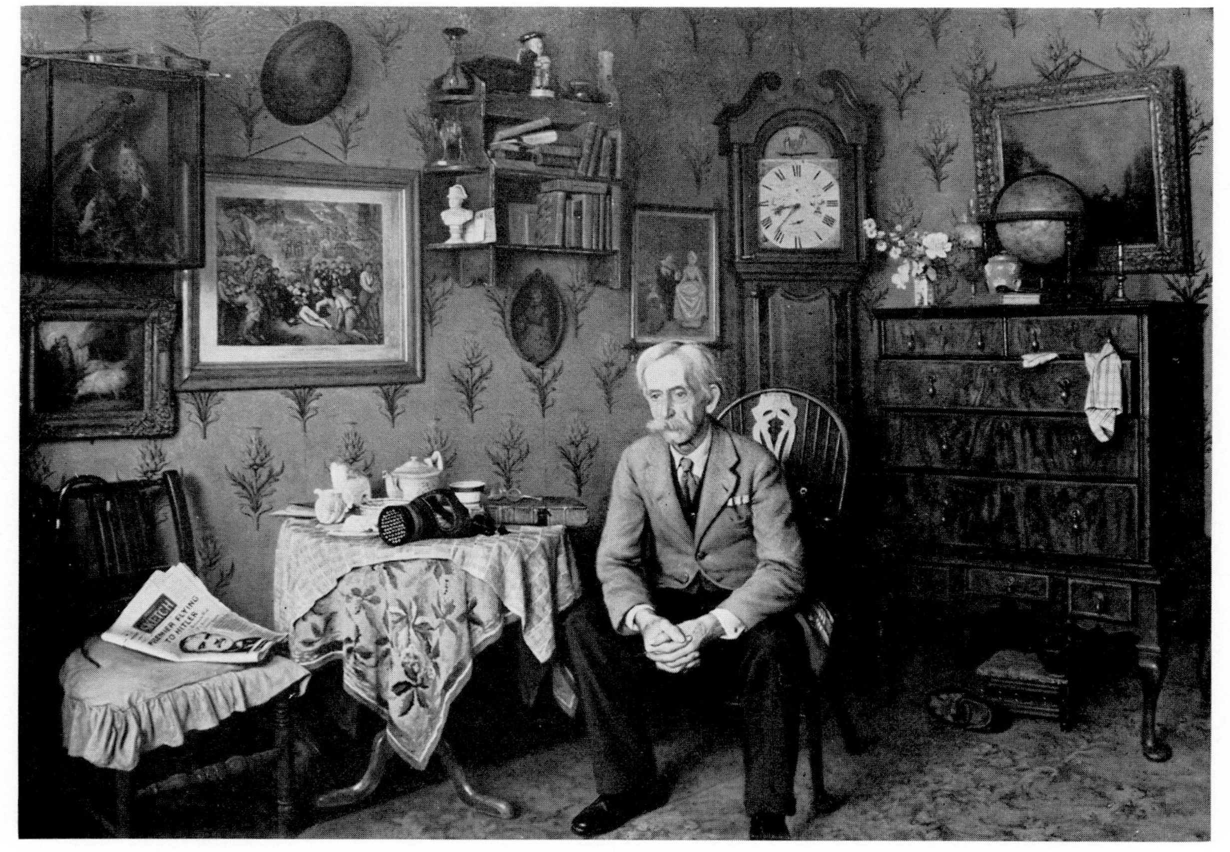

100 'Why War?' by Charles Spencelayh showing in striking fashion the charm of simple wallpaper design in the domestic scene

101 Typical of the Japanese feeling which became popular in wallpaper design during the 1920 period

The excellent condition of many of these papers is partly owing to the fact that the old method of applying wallpapers is quite different to the present one. The old method was to fasten a wooden framework over the surface of the bare walls; this was fixed to wooden wedges driven into the brick or stonework, thus leaving an air space between. On these frames canvas was stretched, and on to this canvas the wallpapers were fixed. It is for this reason that, in many cases, it has been possible to remove them.

1914 ANN WENTWORTH, *House Beautiful*, p. 153, 'Decorative Wallpapers'.

1914 HENRI CLOUZOT, *Gazette des Beaux Arts* (December), 'Le Papier Peint a l'Époque Impériale'.

1914 MACIVER PERCIVAL, *Queen*, pp. 136–56, 'Wall Coverings of Bye-gone Days'.

1915 BOCOCK'S NUTSHELL GUIDE. A tourist's pamphlet which includes a reference to the old wallpaper at the Manor House, Saltfleet, Lincs.

1915 P. RILEY and FRANK COUSINS, *House Beautiful*, p. 148, 'Landscape Wallpapers'.

1916 C. O. MASTERS, 'Wallpapers and their History'. Lecture published in *The Decorator* (January 22).

1916 A. E. SHIPLEY, *Country Life*, 40, 409, 'The Master's Lodgings, Christ's College, Cambridge'.

1916 C. O. MASTERS, *The Decorator* (January 22), 'Wallpapers and their History'.

1916 A. PERRAULT-DABOT, *Bulletin de la Société de l'Histoire de Paris*, Vol. XLIII. 'Un papier de tenture gravé et peint à Paris au XVIIIe siecle' (Papillon).

1916 Victoria and Albert Museum. (Christmas). Note on Exhibition of Interior Paintings and Wallpaper held at the Museum.

1917 MACIVER PERCIVAL, *The Connoisseur* (February), 'Old Wallpapers' (8 illustrations).

So fashionable were they (Chinese wallpapers), even down to 1772 that the Duchess of Norfolk thought it worth while to imitate them by cutting out butterflies to stick on her walls in a kind of paper mosaic.

1917 HELEN D. BOGAN, *Country Life* (July), 'Old Pictorial Wallpapers'.

1917 OLIVER BRACKETT, *The Connoisseur* (October, No. 52, p. 83), 'English Wallpapers of the 18th century'.

1917 PROFESSOR C. F. WARNER. *Home Decoration* (Werner Laurie Ltd., London). The author dedicates this book to 'The Boys and Girls of America' and writes: '*Probably no element of decoration furnishes so many pitfalls to ensnare the unwary as wallpapers do.*' Under a section entitled '*The Ten Commandments of Decoration*' he includes, '*Thou shalt not kill thy neighbours or thy friends with over decorated wallpapers or oppressive decorations of any kind.*'

1918 GEORGE LELAND HUNTER, *Decorative Textiles* (Philadelphia). Contains a chapter on History and Manufacture of Wallpaper. A very informative contribution, copiously illustrated.

1918 *The Journal of Katherine Mansfield* (Constable, 1927). *Journal 1918. re Hotels.*

. . . The strange door shuts upon the stranger and then I slip down in the sheets, waiting for the shadows to come out of the corners and spin their slow, slow web over the Ugliest Wallpaper of All.

1918 E. CLUTE, *House and Garden* (December), 'Chinese Wallpapers of a Century Ago'.

1918 *House and Garden* (December), 'Old French Wallpaper and Decorations'.

1918 W. J. LOCKE, *The Rough Road.* '. . . *And now, my dear boy,*' said the Dean, by way of peroration, '*you cannot but understand that it is your bounden duty to apply yourself to some serious purpose in life.*' '*I do,*' said Doggie, '*I've been thinking over it for a long time. I'm going to gather material for a history of wallpaper.*' Popular novel of the 1914–18 War, the 1st edn. of which was published this year. In a subsequent chapter it transpires that the hero is one third of the way through his history of wallpaper.

1918 ANATOLE FRANCE, *Le Petit Pierre* (Copyright 1918, by Calmann: Léyy, Paris). Relates to mid-nineteenth century.

C'est là que mon esprit se forma, s'élargit et commenca à se peupler de fantômes . . . c'est entre tes quatres murs étroits, semés de fleurs bleues, que m'apparurent d'abord vagues et lointains, les simulacres effrayants de l'amour et de la beauté.

[Anatole France in this book mentions as many as three or four different wallpapers.]

1919 EDWARD J. DUNN, *The History of Wallpaper as a Decoration.* Paper read to New Jersey State Association of Master Painters and Decorators.

1920 MACIVER PERCIVAL, *Old English Furniture and its Surroundings, Restoration to Regency* (London).

1920 GRACE L. TEMPLE, *American Magazine of Art* (September), 'Hunting Old Time Wallpapers'.

1920 HENRI CLOUZOT, *La Renaissance de l'Art Français* (September), 'Au Temps où les Murs Parlaient'.

1920 *Country Life*, Vol. 48, p. 475, 'Chinese Wallpapers'.

1920 *The Wallpaper Magazine.* A House Journal published bi-monthly by The Wall Paper Manufacturers Ltd. First issue was published in April of this year and thereafter was continued without interruption until just before the 1939–45 War began. Contained articles of general interest to wallpaper distributors in this country.

1920 HARALD AARS, *New Norwegian Wallpapers.* Foreningen Brukskunst Årbok, Year Book, 1920.

1920 *Ideal Home Magazine* (London). First published this year since when it has continuously published practical articles on Interior Decoration with special reference to wallpaper.

1921 The House of Heffer Scott & Co, *Romance in Colour and Design.* An advertising brochure describing the development of this London wallpaper business from 1796 to this date.

1921 H. A. TIPPING, *English Homes,* 9 Vols. (London 1921–37). Many references to the use of wallpaper in stately homes.

1921 HERBERT JEANS, *The Periods of Interior Decoration.* Contains a good concluding chapter by METFORD WARNER on 'The Progress of Paper-hangings in England'.

1921 EDWARD B. ALLEN. *House Beautiful,* p. 369, 'Ye Olde Picture Wallpapers'.

1921 HANSARD (June 13). Question to the President of the Board of Trade on the subject of restrictive practices within the wallpaper industry which brought a reassuring reply from Mr. Stanley Baldwin.

1921 H. H. F. JAYNE. *Pennsylvania Museum Bulletin,* Vol. 17, No. 69, p. 6; and No. 71, p. 16. 'The Captain Cook Wallpaper'.

1921 HELEN and JOHN GLOAG, *Simple Furniture and Arrangement* (Duckworth). General references to wallpaper.

1921 CHRISTIAN KOREN-WIBERG, *The Bergen Culture History,* Bergen.

1922 GUSTAVE E. PAZAUREK. *Die Tapete* (Stuttgart). A useful historical account of wallpaper, copiously illustrated in colour and half-tone.

1922 G. WHITELEY WARD, *Wallpaper* (Sir Isaac Pitman & Sons Ltd. London). An interesting account of the origin and manufacture of wallpaper.

> *Some people like lace upon their room walls, and there can be no doubt that if suitable patterns are selected a certain effect of delicacy and richness is obtained . . . Lace wallpaper owes its origin to one, James Sneddon of St. Louis, U.S.A. and as a matter of fact this material has always enjoyed a better vogue in the land of the Stars and Stripes than in our older-fashioned England.*

1922 W. G. P. TOWNSEND, *Modern Decorative Art in England,* Vol. 1, p. 114 (Batsford). A good chapter containing many illustrations of current wallpapers.

> *Mr. Shand Kydd has created for himself a special niche in the wallpaper industry. His designs display an individual outlook and combine artistic judgment with freshness of thought. They are such that give a room an air of distinction and completeness which calls for no further competing enrichment.*

1922 *The Statist* (probably late 1922), 'The Trust Movement in British Industry'. The Wallpaper Combine.

1922 MACIVER PERCIVAL. *The Connoisseur* (January), 'Jackson of Battersea and his Wallpapers'.

1922 MARGARET JOURDAIN. *The Connoisseur* (March), 'Some Early Printed Papers'.

1922 *L'Architecture* (April). 'Le Papier Peint à travers les Ages'.

1922 *Gazette des Beaux Arts*, 'Papiers Peints de l'Époque Napoliénne'.

1922 W. STEWART GREENE. *Architect's Journal* (September). 'Chinese Wallpapers'.

1922 W. K. WATKINS. *Old Time, New England*, Vol. 12, January, p. 109. 'Early Use and Manufacture of Paperhangings in Boston'.

1922 PHYLLIS ACKERMAN. *Arts and Decoration*, Vol. 17, pp. 100, 138, 140, 'Wallpapers in Early American Homes.' [See below.]

1922 G. L. HUNTER. *Good Furniture*, Vol. 19, July, p. 27, 'Early American Wallpapers'.

1922 A. T. BOLTON, *Architecture of Robert and James Adam*. Many references to wallpaper and interesting illustrations.

1923 MARGARET JOURDAIN, *English Interiors in Smaller Houses, 1660–1830* (Batsford). Brief reference to wallpaper on p. 135.

1923 PHYLLIS ACKERMAN, *Wallpaper, Its History, Design, and Use* (Tudor Publishing Co., London and New York). 8° Profusely Illustrated. (A useful Source Book.)

Extract from Preface: *Wallpaper is an important decorative art because, if for no other reason, it is so ubiquitous. Because of its general use it is one of the most important arts for general education in design. Bad wallpaper can do more than any other decorative art to stultify taste; good, to stimulate it.*

1923 NANCY V. MCCLELLAND. *Arts and Decoration* (November), XX, p. 59, 'The Inventors of Wallpapers', Reference to Dominotiers.

1923 TAPESTRY. H. GOBEL, *Wandteppiche*, 6 Vols. Leipsic.

1923 *Manchester Guardian Commercial* (February 15). 'British Progress in Wallpaper Design'.

1924 NANCY V. MCCLELLAND, *Historic Wallpapers* (Philadelphia). With an Introduction by Henri Clouzot, in 4°; 124 illustrations; 12 plates in colour. Specially interesting on French aspect. The introduction by H. Clouzot is a charming literary composition.

When Kate Sanborn collected and published 83 photographs of famous papers in 1905, she rendered a service to lovers of old wallpaper that will never be forgotten. 'If a book has ever been written on this subject,' she said at the time, 'it has been impossible to discover.' Since then so much has been written about wallpaper that it is purely conjectural that there seems still to be room for a book that is purely fact. Except for Felix Follot's report on French wallpapers done for the Retrospective Exhibit at the Paris Exposition of 1900, there has never been a serious scholarly attempt to make a study of this subject from original documents.

1924 B.B.C. BIRMINGHAM. Broadcast talk by B. I. ASTON (June 12) entitled '1924 Wall Decorations'. A very good general survey of the wallpapers of the period.

1924 W. RETERA, *Behangsel en bespanningsstoffen.*

1924 L. MOUSSINAC, *Étoffes imprimées et papiers peints.*

1924 A. V. SUGDEN, *The Crace Papers.* A Paper read to the Institute of British Decorators (December 11). [See 1939 below.]

1924 H. G. DOWLING, *Modern Considerations attaching to Wallpaper Decoration.* A Paper read to the Institute of British Decorators (February 7).

1924 J. PILLEMENT, *Fleurs, Oiseaux, et Fantaisies.* H. Ernst, editeur (Paris). Mostly reproductions of the work of this inventive designer.

1924 BASIL IONIDES. *Architectural Review*, 56, 195, 'Wallpaper in a Sixteenth-Century House'.

1924 MARGARET JOURDAIN. *Country Life* (May). 'Old English Wallpapers and Wall Hangings', Illustrated.

There was a revival of interest in Chinese papers during the Regency perhaps as a reaction against the severities of the Greek manner, and in 1802 some fine Chinese papers were given to the Prince Regent who formed a gallery at the Pavilion at Brighton decorated with dragons, lanterns and pagodas to show off his treasure to the best advantage.

1924 PIERRE GUSMAN, *Byblis*, No. IX, pp. 18–23. 'J. B. Michel-Papillon et ses Papiers de Tenture'.

1924 NANCY MCCLELLAND, *Antiques* (September), Vol. 6, No. 3, p. 138. 'The Washington Memorial Paper'.

1924 MARY WEBB, *Precious Bane* (Cape, first published, 1924). Famous novel of Shropshire life in early nineteenth century.

So I'd bought a few rolls of cheap paper out of the butter money and I was papering it unbeknown to Gideon; Mother was in the secret, and she'd come and clasp her hands and say, 'Looks a pretty paper! Doing it right well you are, my dear. Roses and all! Roses be lucky to my mind. Your aunt Dorcas had roses in her bride chamber, and not one of her children ever died, nor ailed, nor cried!'

1924 ELEANOR MORDAUNT (Short Stories), *People, Houses and Ships* (Hutchinson & Co.), under the title 'Four Wallpapers' the author tells a story of haunting by wallpaper. The action takes place in a house in Spain.

Funny old things as they were, there was something in them; not the pattern, more than that—something which touched her—appealed to her; some feeling of the life which they had once surrounded, the tastes they had gratified. 'There were people who liked us once,' they seemed to say.

1925 DUCHARTE et SAULNIER, *L'Imagerie Populaire* (Paris). 40, 34 pl. colour.

1925 *The Journal of Decorative Art.* Three very useful articles by MACIVER PERCIVAL (July, Sept., Oct.). English Wallpapers of the Chippendale and Sheraton periods, etc.

1925 H. G. DOWLING, *Wallpaper, Its History, Production and Possibilities.* A thoughtful and constructive Paper read to the Royal Society of Arts (March 25).

1925 *The House Beautiful Furnishing Annual.* (Published by The Atlantic Monthly Company, Boston, U.S.A.). Contains an article (p. 17) on Wallpaper probably written by Nancy McClelland.

1925 *Country Life*, No. 57, 'Chippendale and Wallpaper'.

1925 HENRI CLOUZOT. *Renaissance de l'Art Français* (April). 'Le Papier Peint au début du XVIII° siècle. A l'Enseigne du Papillon'.

1925 HILARY JENKINSON, M.A., F.S.A. *The Antiquaries Journal*, Vol.V, No. 3. 'English Wallpapers of the 16th and 17th centuries'. A very useful contribution to the study of old wallpaper.

The subject of early wallpapers has not been much investigated in England. Of the various forms of wall decoration which preceded them—painted, stencilled or incised designs, hangings of plain material, tapestry, embroidery, cloth stained or painted, importations from China, scenic papers —of all these something is known, though we still wait for an authoritative work. But little attempt has been made so far to bridge the gap between mediaeval and modern, the sixteenth and the eighteenth centuries.

1925 NANCY MCCLELLAND, *Decorative Wall Treatments* (Lippincott, New York).

1926 A. V. SUGDEN and J. L. EDMONDSON, *A History of English Wallpaper—1509–1914*, 70 pl. col.; 190 illustrations (Batsford). Standard work on the subject and containing a section giving the history of all the most important wallpaper mills in this country. Also section on Relief Materials, such as Anaglypta, Lincrusta, etc. (An indispensable source book.)

Extract from Foreword: *The scope of the book is as comprehensive as it has been practicable to make it. Beginning with the first crude attempts to use paper bearing a design or picture as a form of decoration in substitution for the costly gilt embossed leathers and figured textiles of the period, the development in technical and artistic achievement is traced down to the year 1914.*

1926 For 1926 period see ALDOUS HUXLEY, *Eyeless in Gaza*, published 1936.

1926 W. H. CANTRILL and W. G. SUTHERLAND, *Paperhanging.* An instructional hand-book issued by Sutherland Publishing Co., Manchester.

1926 NANCY MCCLELLAND. *The Practical Book of Decorative Wall Treatments* (Philadelphia).

1926 HILARY JENKINSON, M.A., F.S.A. Another lecture on sixteenth and seventeenth-century Wallpapers, this time delivered at Stationers' Hall, London, E.C. [See above.]

1926 *Illustrated London News* (March 20). Review of A. V. Sugden's book [see above]. There were many interesting reviews of this book at and after the date of publication, but in most cases very little new to the subject came out of them. (*Continued on page 159*)

102 Typical machine printed floral wallpaper of the interwar period. Designed by J. H. Gibbons and produced by A. Sanderson & Sons Ltd, about 1925

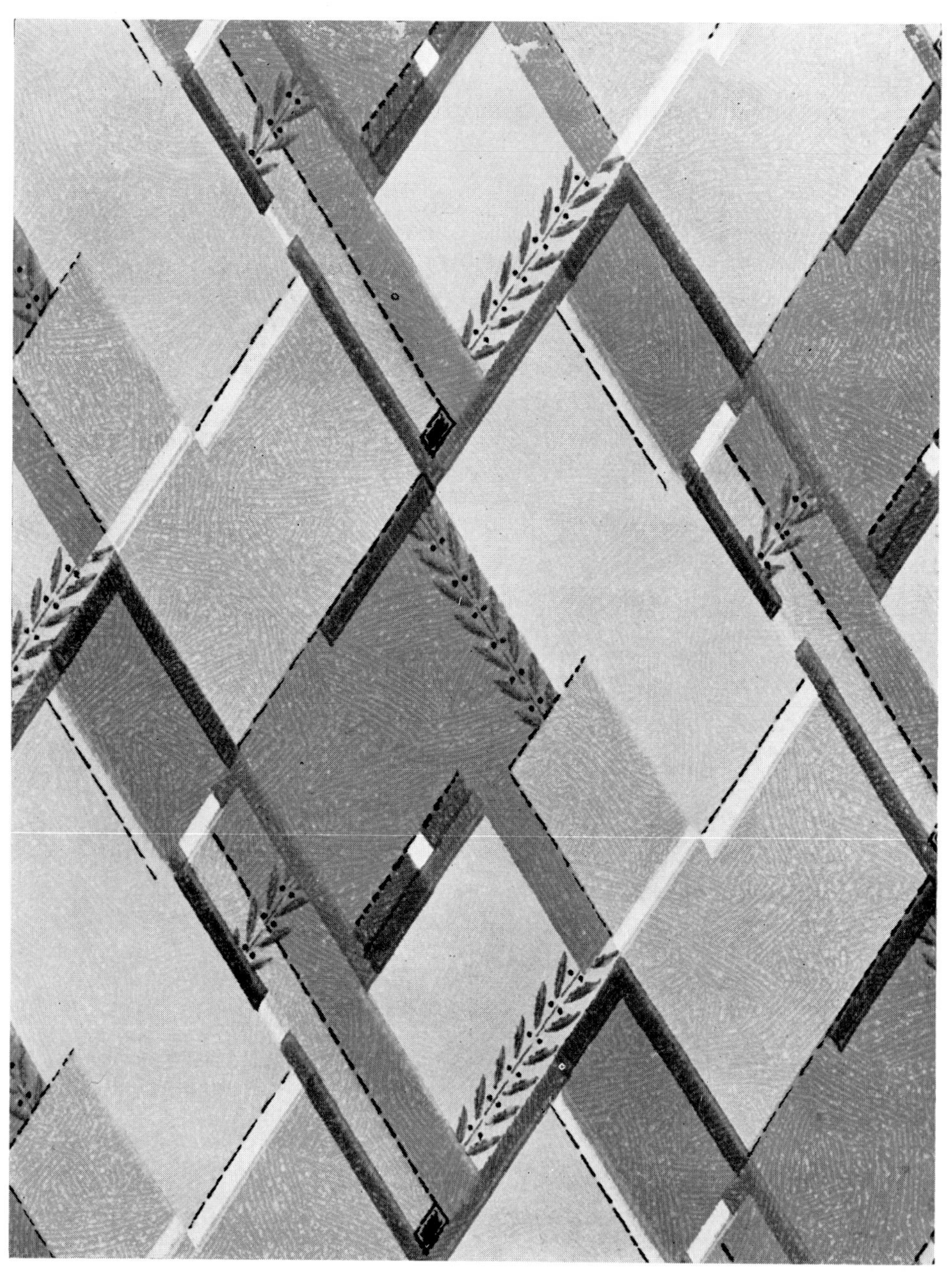

103 English machine printed wallpaper reflecting the cubist trend of the 1930's

Therein lies the secret of successful papering: the transforming of the dingy into the delightful. The rest is progress in design, in colouring, more particularly in colours that will never fly off—in durability, in cheapness, thanks be to mechanical genius, to increasing artistry acknowledging Morris and the rest—and to the master paperstainers.

1926 EUGENE CLUTE, *The Treatment of Interiors* (New York). Contains an interesting chapter on p. 143: 'Old Wallpapers'.

1926 *The Connoisseur*, 'Picture Backgrounds'. Notes by Arthur Sanderson and Sons on the Decoration of the National Art Galleries. (Arthur Sanderson & Sons, Ltd., 55, Berners Street, W.1.)

1927 PAGET TOYNBEE, M.A., *Strawberry Hill Accounts, 1747–1795.* Notes and Index. Oxford. Clarendon Press. Only 500 copies printed.

Extract from p. 39 *Note on Wallpapers. . . . the use of wallpapers was a new fashion at this time. In his letter of Mar. 4, 1753. Walpole tells Mann: 'I went the other morning with Mr. Conway to buy some of the new furniture paper for you: if there was any money at Florence, I should expect this manufacture would make its fortune there.*

1927 C. C. OMAN. *Old Furniture*, Vol. I (June–September) to Vol. IV (May–August, 1928). Four successive articles: (1) Black and White Papers; (2) Early Coloured Papers; (3) Chinese Papers; (4) Later Coloured Papers and Print Rooms. Illustrated.

1927 *La Renaissance de l'Art Français* (February). 'L'Atelier du Cartier-Dominotier'.

1927 Canada's Wallpaper Magazine commenced. Vol. 1, No. 1. Extract from 'Editorial Whittlings' which contains an unusually reverent statement:

Wallpaper is now as never before, an artistic production. It furnishes the home, it brings it beauty and dignity, it enhances the prestige of the inmates, it promotes health and vigour.

1927 C. C. OMAN. *Country Life*, LXII, No. 1599, p. 40. 'Old English Flock Papers'.

1927 SELLING, G., *Hur gammal är stofttapeten* (Stockholm).

1927 BASIL MORTIMER. *The Industrial World* (August). 'The Romance of Business' (contains a reference to Hayward & Son Ltd., London).

1928 CORDONNIER-DETRIE, *Jacques Gaugain, Cartier-Dominotier en la ville du Mans au 18° siècle* (Le Mans), 8°, plates.

1928 *Old Furniture*, Vol. III, p. 17, 'Coutts Bank Chinese Paper'.

1928 HENRI CLOUZOT. *La Renaissance de l'Art Français*, Vol. II, pp. 377–383. 'Outillage moderne du papier peint'.

1928 Musée Galliéra, Paris. Illustrated catalogue of the Exposition de Toile Imprimée et Papier Peint. Most of the big French manufacturers participated.

1928 NANCY MCCLELLAND. *La Renaissance de l'Art Français,* Vol. XI, No. 5, p. 207. 'Papiers peint Français dans les demeures Américaines'.

1928 MARIE LOUISE LE VERRIER. *Antiques,* Vol. XIII, No. 2, p. 1,237. 'Old Wallpapers of France'.

1928 HENRI CLOUZOT. *L'Opinion,* Vol. 21, No. 35, p. 15. 'Le Papier Peint Révolutionnaire'.

1928 E. M. FORSTER. *Goldsworthy Lowes Dickinson* (Edward Arnold & Co.), 1934. Describing Dickinson's rooms at Cambridge (about 1928 period) which had been decorated under the advice of ROGER FRY, the author of this biography states:

The second main room looked over the Backs. Its walls had a grass paper of grey green and on the floor was a Chinese carpet featuring four thin pale-purple dragons on a biscuit-coloured ground.

1929 C. C. OMAN, M.A., *Catalogue of Wallpapers* (in Victoria and Albert Museum). Published under the Authority of the Board of Education. A very full and scholarly account of the advent and development of wallpaper. 29 Illustrations, Index of Designers, Manufacturers, etc.

1929 ELIZABETH BOWEN, *Joining Charles* (Jonathan Cape).

It was a smallish room with sloping ceilings, and a faded paper rambled over by roses. . . .

1929 AUGUSTE MARTIN, *L'Imagerie Orléanaise, precedée d'une étude de P. L. Duchartre, notices biographiques du Dr. Garsonnin,* Orléans. 4° fig. et pl. en couleurs.

1929 RENÉ CHARANCE. *Le Papier Peint et le décor de la Maison.*

1929 Lecture on Wallpaper Printing given by C. O. MASTERS. Part of a series of lectures on printing, sponsored by The Stationers' Company, London. This paper deals with a number of aspects of the subject including a derisory account of the efforts of amateur decorators. The Lecturer said:

All the amateur can say at the finish of his attempt is: 'Well, it's all my own work'; and the reply of course, will be, 'It looks like it!'

1929 E. A. ENTWISLE, *Painting and Decorating,* 6 Vols. Illustrated. (Pitman, London).Vol. III, Section IX. Section on History and Manufacture of Wallpaper.

1929 NANCY MCCLELLAND. *Encyclopaedia Britannica.* 14 Edn. Under 'Interior Decoration' 'Wallpaper', an illustrated article.

1929 *Art et Industrie* (January, March, May), 'Les Grandes Époques du Papier Peint'.

1929 *Cabinet Maker and Complete House Furnisher* (London, July 13), 'Historical Wallpapers'. Review of C. C. OMAN's *Catalogue.* [See above.]

1929 W. GURNEY BENHAM. *The Essex Review,* 'Wall Decorations, Paintings and Paper'. Relates to a discovery of old wallpaper at Holly Trees Mansion, Colchester. [See 1930.]

1929 GRACE LINCOLN TEMPLE. *Antiques*, Vol. 15, No. 4 (U.S.A.). 'The Story of Wallpaper'.

1929 HENRI CLOUZOT, *Papiers Peints et Tentures Modernes*, Paris. Description of the way in which wallpaper and furnishing fabrics have progressed from the eighteenth century to this date.

1930 *Les chef d'œuvres du papier peint: Tableaux-Tentures de Dufour et Leroy* (Paris). Folio, 54 plates in half tone and colour. With an interesting introduction by Henri Clouzot.

1930 C. H. EWING. *Instruction Manual for Paperhangers*. McGraw Hill Vocational Texts (New York).

1930 EUGÈNE DABIT, *L'Hotel du Nord* (novel).

... Une lumière grise s'accrochait aux rideaux déchirés, un papier à fleurs déteint attristait les murs ...

1930 HILARY JENKINSON, M.A., F.S.A. *A recently discovered Wallpaper at Colchester*. [See Essex Review 1929 above.] Read before Essex Archaeological Society, and printed in the *Essex Archaeol. Transactions*, Vol. XIX, part 4.

1930 TAPESTRY. W. G. THOMSON, *A History of Tapestry* (London).

1930 J. M. BARRIE, *The Greenwood Hat* (Peter Davies), Chapter XIV. Whimsical reference to 'educational wallpapers and their effect on a child of six'

An apocryphal biography: '*Here am I, at the age of six years, so full of learning that yesterday I had a grey hair. ... I spend much of my life between historical wallpapers.*'

1931 HENRI CLOUZOT, *Le papier peint en France du 17e au 19° siecle*. 36 pp., 32 plates (Paris).

1931 EDNA DONNELL, 'The Van Rensselaer Painted Wallpaper'. *Bulletin of The Metropolitan Museum of Art*, (New York), Vol. XXVI, December, Section 2, pp. 10–16. [See also 1932 below.]

1931 HENRI CLOUZOT, *La Renaissance de l'Art Français*, Vol. 10, No. 3, p. 83. 'L'Atelier du Cartier—Dominotier.'

1931 DENTON WELCH. Written in 1945 but referring to an earlier period when he fled from Repton School.

I got into the white bed and lay down to sleep. It was a horrible night. I kept on waking up so that my dreams were mixed up with the wallpaper, and somehow the Virgin Mary appeared and disappeared dressed all in Reckitt's Blue.

1931 LIONEL CUFFE. (John Betjeman). *Architectural Review* (May). 'William Morris'. Actual hand-printed wallpaper interleaved with the following inscription printed on the back: "*The Bower*"—*A hand-blocked wallpaper designed by William Morris—This is one of William Morris's early designs and consists of a close tangle of flower forms and leaves in which pink tulips and garden lilies are conspicuous ... etc.*

Two other actual wallpapers are bound into this issue: 'The Powdered', hand-printed wallpaper designed about 1870. 'The Daisy', Morris's design—the first to appear.

Betjeman says of these:

They are almost the last good papers to be designed by an artist. Later, the task of inventing them was left to weary art students and commercial hacks! They designed the wallpapers with which we were to surround ourselves. It is small wonder that plain walls and distemper have for long been popular and that wallpapers are only just being rediscovered as a great chance for good designers.

Also: *We may not be able to wade through 'The Earthly Paradise' but we can understand his colours and his mind through his lyrics. And in his designs for paper, especially, he has written his lyrics for a second time. These papers are not only a proof that artist and manufacturer combined can produce good and lasting work. Less than a hundred years ago, Morris and Burne Jones, Philip Webb and Ernest Gimson were inspired by an idea that artist and manufacturer should be one and the same thing; or friends, at any rate. Since then in England they have generally been enemies . . .*

In the same issue appears the concluding article on 'A History of the English House' by Nathaniel Lloyd—the previous articles appearing in *The Architectural Review* for January–July, October, November, 1928; January–May, October–December, 1929; January–April, June, July, October–December, 1930; February and April, 1931. Interesting notes on Wallpaper. See also Nathaniel Lloyd, *History of the House*, in book form. Architectural Press.

1932 EDNA DONNELL, 'The Van Rensselaer Wallpaper and J. B. Jackson. A Study in Disassociation'. 33 pp. 32 illustrations. *Metropolitan Museum of Art Studies* (New York), Vol. IV, Part 1. Illustrated. An interesting monograph on the subject of J. B. Jackson, paperstainer of London during the eighteenth century.

1932 F. R. S. YORKE, F.R.I.B.A. *Architectural Review* (February). A critical article on current trends of design.

1932 C. C. OMAN. *Fine Arts* (December). 'Wallpapers made in England, 1760–1800'.

1932 MRS. W. HODGSON. *The Connoisseur* (July). 'Chinese Wallpaper at Coutt's Bank'.

1932 C. C. OMAN. *The Connoisseur* (October). 'An unusual Charles II Wallhanging'. An article describing mural decorations discovered in 1931 at Ivy House, Worcester.

1932 *Journal of Decorative Art* (March). Article regarding a Victorian decorator and paperstainer, viz. R. Horne, Gracechurch St., London.

1932 MACIVER PERCIVAL. *The Antique Collector* (August). 'In the Indian Taste'. Article on Chinese wallpapers.

1932 HENRI CLOUZOT, *Le papier peint à Lyon et dans la region. La Soierie de Lyon*, Vol. 15, No. 12, p. 298.

104 Realistic treatment of natural form: a machine printed English wallpaper, *c.*1930

H. CLOUZOT ET CH. FOLLOT

HISTOIRE
DU
PAPIER PEINT
EN FRANCE

PRÉFACE
PAR
JEAN BOURGUIGNON

PARIS
ÉDITIONS D'ART CHARLES MOREAU
8, RUE DE PRAGUE
—
1935

105 Title page of Clouzot and Follot's monumental book on the history of wallpaper, published in Paris, 1935

1933 A. V. SUGDEN. *The Book of British Industries* (London). Chapter on Wallpaper.

In 1770 the production of wallpaper in England was about 250,000 pieces and the duty paid was £13,000. In 1834 over £63,000 was paid in duty representing 1,200,000 pieces. In 1860 the production was 19 millions and in 1874 it was 32 millions. Today the annual output in England is nearly three times that figure and the pieces produced if joined end to end would pass round the circumference of the earth about twenty or thirty times.

1933 JOHNSON'S *England* (Oxford University Press), Vol. II. Useful article by OLIVER BRACKETT, 'The Interior of the House'.

1933 C. C. OMAN. *Country Life* (February). 'English Chinoiserie Wallpapers'.

Chinese wallpapers began to reach this country late in the 17th century, and were immediately imitated.

1933 *The Decorator* (June 15). 'A XVIIth-Century Lining Paper'.

1933 LEWIS F. DAY, *Pattern Design* (Batsford). *A Book for Students treating in a practical way of the anatomy, planning and evolution of repeated ornament.* Of special interest to the wallpaper designer. 8vo. 2nd Edn. Illustrated.

1933 *The Antique Collector* (October). 'Chinese Wallpapers' by PRUNUS. Illustrated.

1933 F. K. HASCALL, *Harry Wearne and his Work* (New York). Illustrated in colour. Harry Wearne was an Englishman who went to France in 1880 and became designer and colourist for the famous wallpaper firm, Zuber & Co.: Rixheim, Alsace, later designed fabrics in America.

1933 W. M. WEBB. *West Middlesex Gazette* (May 13). 'Wallpaper making'. Reference to Sandersons, Perivale. Illustrated.

1933 Musée Galliéra, Paris. *Exposition historique de l'aéronotique et rétrospectif de papier peints.* Catalogue, November 1933 to January 1934. Illustrated. Commemorative Exhibition doubtless inspired by Réveillon's (French wallpaper maker) interest in his friend's (Montgolfier) experiments in ballooning. [See 1783 above.]

1934 E. A. ENTWISLE. *The Connoisseur* (June). 'Painted Chinese Wallpapers'.

1934 G. H. CROW. *The Studio* (Special Winter Number). 'William Morris, Designer'.

1934 *Antiques* (U.S.A.) (March). 'Wallpaper Editions of the *Vicksburg Daily Citizen*, by HENRY S. PARSONS. Historical account of an occasion during the American Civil War when, owing to shortage of newsprint, this newspaper was printed on the back of wallpaper. An article on this subject appeared in the *Journal of Decorative Art*, 1940. [See also *Wallpaper Newspapers of the Civil War*, by CLARENCE BRIGHAM. Harvard University Press.]

1934 ETHEL MANNIN, *Men are Unwise*. Theme of this novel is based on experiences of the author while working with Charles F. Higham Ltd. who were at this period advertising agents for a large firm of wallpaper manufacturers.

1934 MAURICE GRUIN, *Manuel de l'Industrie et du Commerce du Papier Peint* (Paris).

1935 HENRI CLOUZOT et CHARLES FOLLOT, *Histoire du Papier Peint en France*. Preface by Jean Bourguignon. (Moreau, Paris.) pp. 272. Numerous illustrations in colour and half tone. Monumental volume representing a great deal of research on the subject. Equivalent in importance to Sugden & Edmondson's standard work published in 1926.

1935 *Architectural Review* (October). Vol. 78, p. 140. 'German Wallpaper Museum at Kassel.'

1935 ANINE WOLLEBŒK SLAATTO. 'The Wallpapers at Lysgård', *Art and Culture*, 21, pp. 134–6.

1936 HENRI CLOUZOT, *Tableaux Tentures de Dufour et Leroy*.

1936 The Wall Paper Manufacturers Ltd. *Wallpaper*. Interesting illustrated book dealing generally with the subject and containing 13 specimens of embossed wallpaper.

1936 E. A. ENTWISLE. *The Connoisseur* (January). 'Early Black and White Papers'.

1936 ANDRÉ CARLHIAN, *Panoramic Wallpapers*. Illustrated. Informed description of these French papers.

> *... Ces tableaux sont en camaïeu ou en couleurs et la nécessité d'utiliser une planche par couleur, ainsi que les dimensions réduites de ces planches provoquaient leur multiplication et tel papier comporte plus de 3,000 planches.*

1936 EWART DUDLEY. *The Connoisseur* (August). 'Bay of Naples Wallpaper'.

1936 ALDOUS HUXLEY, *Eyeless in Gaza*. (Chatto & Windus, 1936.)

Extract relating to the 1926 period:—

> *... Mark lived in a dingy house off the Fulham Road. Dark, brown brick with terra-cotta trimmings; and within, patterned linoleum; bits of red Axminster carpet; wallpapers of ochre sprinkled with bunches of cornflowers, of green, with crimson roses; fumed oak chairs and tables; rep curtains; bamboo stands supporting glazed blue pots. The hideousness, Anthony reflected, was so complete ... that it could only have been intentional.*

1937 NICKOLAUS PEVSNER, *An Enquiry into Industrial Art in England*. Reference to Wallpapers, p. 67.

1937 A. S. JENNINGS, *Modern Painter and Decorator*. Revised. Vols. 1–3 inclusive.

106 Hand printed wallpaper, 'Royal Oak', designed by John Aldridge, A.R.A., for Cole & Son (Wallpapers) Ltd, 1938

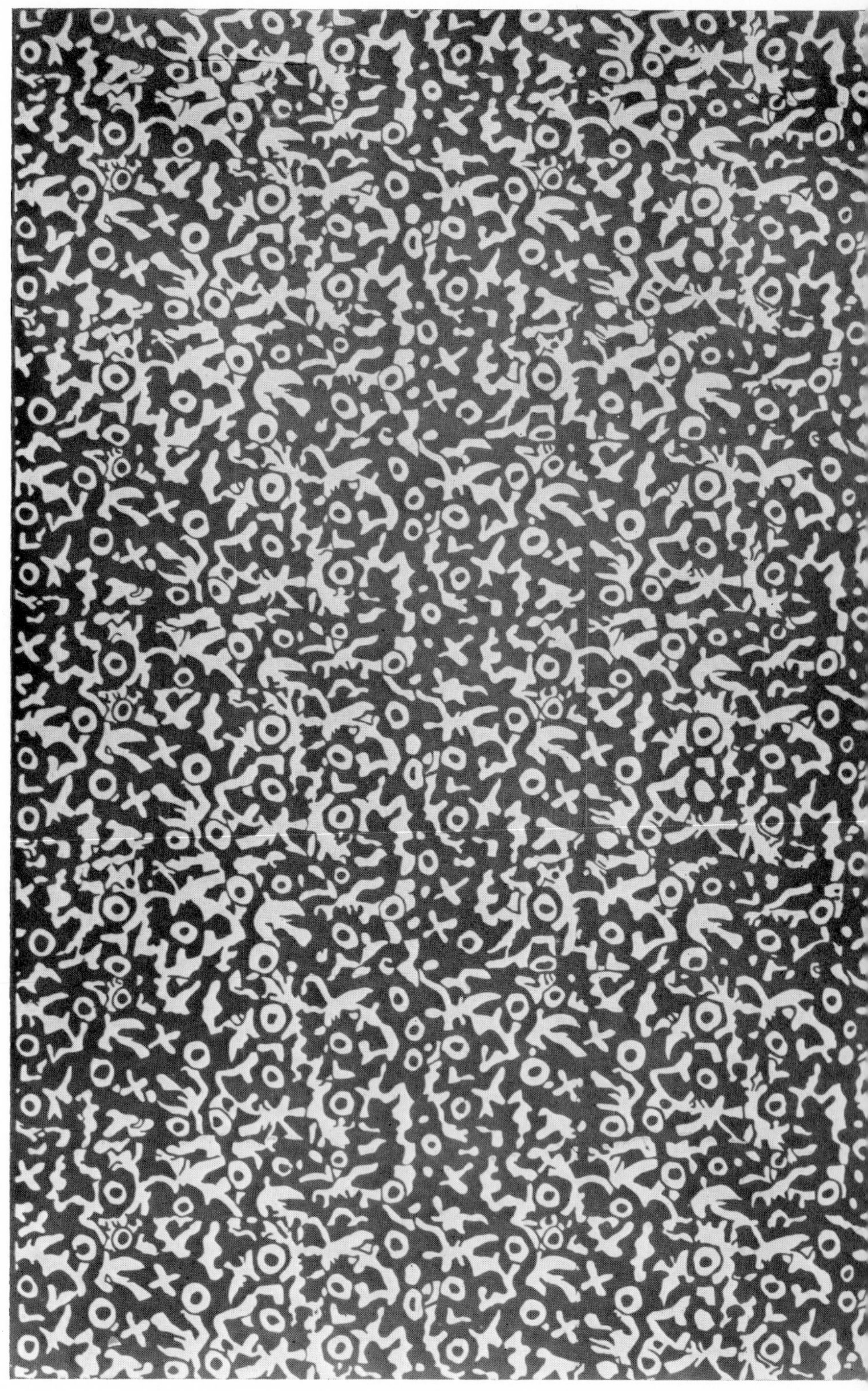

107 Wallpaper design by Graham Sutherland produced by Cole & Son (Wallpapers) Ltd

1937 *C.I.B.A. Review* (No. 3, November). Published by The Society of Chemical Industries, Basle. Contents:

The History of Mural Hangings, GRETE DE FRANCESCO, Milan, p. 70.
Wallpapers, GRETE DE FRANCESCO, p. 75.
Birds and Beasts in Wallpaper, GRETE DE FRANCSESCO, p. 93.
The History of Wallpapers in England, J. H. SMITH, p. 96.
Modern Wallpaper Manufacture, M. C. NEUBURGER, Vienna, p. 102.
Historical Gleanings, p. 104.

This is an authoritative pamphlet on wallpaper and one which is well worth consulting. Very detailed and accurate. The numerous illustrations are well selected and unusual at this date—though some have clearly been gleaned from Sugden and Edmondson's book of 1926.

1937 *De Geschiedenis van het Papieren Behangsel de Directie van Rath & Doodeheefver*. Cultural Historical review of the development of the Wallpaper Industry by PROFESSOR MACHMAR. Catalogue of an Exhibition in Holland (October 20).

1937 LEATHER HANGINGS. *The Burlington Magazine* (July). 'English Chinoiserie Gilt Leather', HANS HUTH. Illustrated. Informative account of the London leather gilders some of whom later became paperhanging makers.

The seat of this London Industry seems to have been almost entirely in or near St. Paul's Churchyard. As the leather gilders did not belong to the Leather Sellers' Company and probably did not form a guild of their own it is not possible to examine their records, so we can only refer to a few advertisements, trade cards, etc.

1937 H. E. KEYES. *Antiques* (U.S.A.). Vol. 31, No. 2. 'The Editor's Attic—a Washington Memorial Wallpaper'.

1937 E. G. PAULUS. *Gebrauchsgraphik*, Vol. 14, No. 5, p. 24. 'The German Museum of Wallpapers in Kassel'.

1937 LINING PAPERS. A. J. B. WACE, 'Lining Papers from Corpus Christi College', in the Journal *Oxoniensia*, Vol. II, published by the Oxford Architectural and Historical Society. An interesting contribution claiming that the so-called 'black and white' lining papers were probably pattern papers for embroidery, and not imitations of stitch work as many historians have affirmed. [See Hilary Jenkinson, 1925.]

1937-38 Buffalo Fine Arts Academy. Albright Art Gallery. Exhibition of Wallpaper, Historical and Contemporary. December 4–January 16. Buffalo, N.Y. (Illustrated).

In this Exhibition the Albright Art Gallery honours one of Buffalo's oldest industries related to the field of Art, and presents to the general public a survey of one of the industrial arts which contributes largely to the amenities of daily life. The exhibition has been planned to illustrate as completely as possible to the present day, the history of wallpaper design and printing. There are necessarily important omissions, but the classic period of both printing and design, the 18th century in France, is fortunately well represented.

1938 French Scenic Wallpapers. Catalogue of the André Carlhian Collection of Scenic and Panoramic Wallpapers exhibited at Messrs. A. Sanderson & Sons Ltd., Berners Street, London (January 15–16).

Extract from the Introduction: *Although produced during the Revolution and the Wars of the Empire, these papers were freely exported and found their way into England, and especially into America, where in more houses than in any other country examples are still the decoration of important rooms. From the manufacturers' records the names of some of the artists have been recovered including Mader, Charvet, Brock, Deltil, and Laffitte. There is evidence also of the work of Boilly, Debucourt, and Carle Vernet.*

1938 FRANZ RULLMANN, *Die Tapete und ihre Herstellung* (Koch G.M.B.H. Stuttgart). pp. 112. Illustrated. 16 samples. List of German manufacturers, etc. A very comprehensive treatise on the origins and progress of the wallpaper industry in Germany. The first half of this work describes the historical background and the remaining chapters deal mainly with machine technique of the pre-war period. (Johann Becker is mentioned as one who played an important part in developing the wallpaper printing machine as soon as paper in 'endless' lengths became freely available.) [Further edition 1958].

1938 M. SANKEY and M. M'VEAGH REYNOLDS, *Designing for Printed Furnishing Fabrics and Wallpapers* (London).

1938 Cooper Union Museum, New York. (*Chronicle*, Vol. 1, No. 4, April.) Catalogue. Illustrated.

The entire group of wallpapers in the Museum printed before 1900, which has been investigated in the light of fresh information only recently available, is here published in a catalogue accompanied by illustrations of some of the more unusual and noteworthy examples. The history of a distinguished branch of industrial design is well reflected in these documents; but what is equally important, the means of production is not lost from sight. A bibliography accompanying the catalogue indicates sources of information regarding technique, . . etc.

1938 GERMAINE et GEORGES DEGAAST, *Art et Métiers Graphiques*, No. 61, pp. 33–42. 'La Technique de Fabrication du Papier Peint'.

1938 EWART DUDLEY. *The Connoisseur* (August). 'Télémaque en Calypso' (French panoramic wallpaper).

1938 *The Irish Times* (July 30). 'Manufacturing Wallpapers in Ireland' (reference to new mill at Kildare).

1939 A. V. SUGDEN and E. A. ENTWISLE, *Potters of Darwen—a Century of Wallpaper Printing by Machinery*. (Privately printed to mark the centenary of the C. & J. G. Potter Branch of The Wall Paper Manufacturers Ltd.) Pp. 120. Illustrated. A useful source book on the origin and development of wallpaper printing by machine in view of the fact that this mill in Darwen, Lancs. was largely responsible for the introduction of machine-made wallpapers to the world. The book describes this development and includes interesting excerpts from contemporary sources describing wallpaper making one hundred and twenty years ago, and onwards. Foreword by J. L. EDMONDSON.

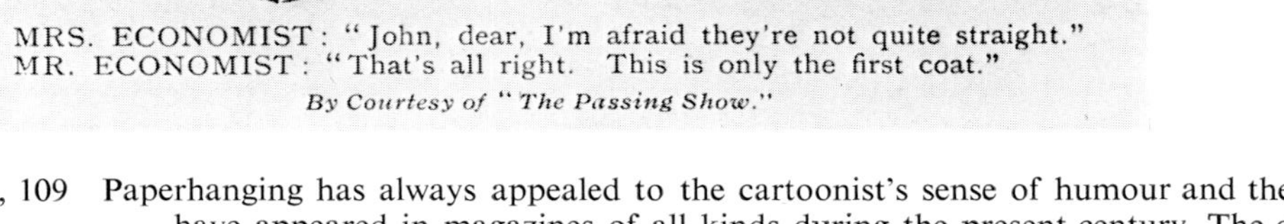

MRS. ECONOMIST: "John, dear, I'm afraid they're not quite straight."
MR. ECONOMIST: "That's all right. This is only the first coat."
By Courtesy of "The Passing Show."

108, 109 Paperhanging has always appealed to the cartoonist's sense of humour and the drawing (left) is typical of many such which have appeared in magazines of all kinds during the present century. The drawing (right) speaks for itself

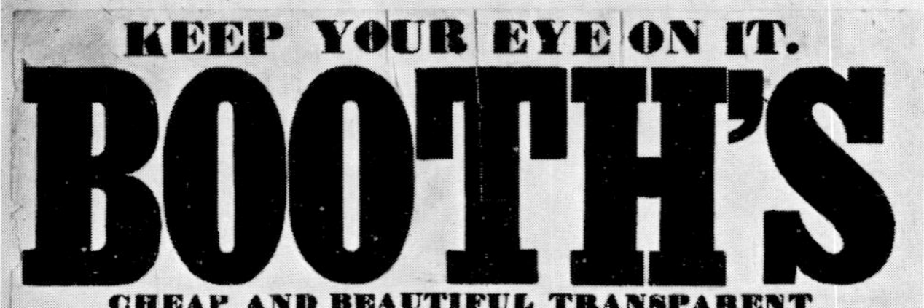

110 Window bill of about 1860 period

111 Poster by Laurence Scarfe, 1945

1939 A. V. SUGDEN and E. A. ENTWISLE, *Notes and Comments on the Paper read to the R.I.B.A. in 1839 by John G. Crace entitled 'A History of Paper-hangings.'* Illustrated.

A Reprint of the two papers read by John Gregory Crace a hundred years ago by the R.I.B.A. seemed desirable to the compilers of this booklet for many reasons. J. G. Crace was the first real historian of the art of paper-staining and the two papers which follow had never been reprinted in full until recently when the present version was published in two succeeding issues of the Record, *the official organ of the Incorporated Institute of British Decorators.*

Useful source book describing the development of wallpaper making as well as early methods of manufacture.

1939 JOHN P. PARRY, *Practical Paperhanging.*

1939 F. J. HARRIS. *Architectural Review* (December). 'Wallpaper'.

1939 OSBERT LANCASTER, *Homes Sweet Homes* (John Murray). Amusing drawings and lively text, this book defines the styles and spirit of domestic interiors from the middle ages to the 1930's.

1939 DECORATED PAPERS. 'Signature'—a Quadrimestrial of Typography and Graphic Arts (July 12). The Hirsch Collection of Decorated Papers by H. P. R. FINBERG. Reference to hand printing from wood blocks, etc. [See also ROSAMUND LORING *Decorative Book Papers*, etc.]

1939 SVEN RYGGE, *Regency Wallpapers at Milde, after a plate print of Berain.* (Annual Report, Norwegian Antiquity Collection, pp. 129–38.)

1939 Cooper Union Museum. *Fundamental Rules for Wallpaper Design*, by WILLIAM E. KATZENBACH. Practical information for the wallpaper designer.

1940 SIR REGINALD BLOMFIELD, R.A., *Richard Norman Shaw* (*Architect, 1831–1912*). (Batsford). Reference to wallpaper as follows:

Mr. Robert Shaw, in his notes on his father says that the latter thought that William Morris, instead of producing expensive textiles and wall-papers should have devoted himself to the manufacture of cheap chests of drawers, and wallpapers at 10½d. a piece. . . . Shaw had very definite views on wallpapers. He insisted that they should be 'backgrounds pure and simple—that and nothing more'. It is disconcerting when you find that your host and hostess are less noticeable than the wallpapers. 'If there is any pattern at all it ought to be of the simplest kind, quite un-obtrusive.' Hinc illae lachrimae; Morris held that the wallpaper should be a beautiful thing itself hence his ambitious and intricate patterns. For myself I always thought his 'powdered paper' was the simplest and far the best of all his papers, and it looked to me as if the pattern was an old one, just small sprays of roses scattered about in a yellow ground, and I think Shaw was right and Morris wrong in this. . . .*

[* R. N. SHAW in *The British Home of Today* (1904).]

c. 1940–50 PHYLLIS ACKERMAN. *Antiques* (*U.S.A.*). 'Wallpapers from New England Houses'. Illustrated.

1941 E. A. ENTWISLE. *Journal of Decorative Art* (November). 'Bromwich of Ludgate Hill'. [See earlier references to this famous paperstainer of the eighteenth century].

1941 *World's Paper Trade Review* (April 25). 'Ancient Wallpaper'. Reference to a French panoramic wallpaper purchased by a British major at about the time of Waterloo.

1941 SIR CHARLES OMAN, *Memories of Victorian Oxford*, Chap. XX. (Referring to the mother of Frederic Myers.)

> *Old Mrs. Myers had a classical Georgian house which had been built for the exiled heir of the Bourbons, the Duc de Berri, about 1808. . . . The interior of the house was pure French 'Empire', there was one room papered with a gorgeous view of the Tuileries Gardens under the 'ancien Régime' with ladies and soldiers promenading . . . a favourite decoration scheme of the time. I often wondered how so much French wallpaper could have been smuggled over to England about the time of the Napoleonic Wars.*

[See 1938 extract from Carlhian Exhibition Catalogue.]

1941 EIVIND S. ENGELSTAD, *Statsråd Petterson's 'Soellie', the later Bervens Lôkke*. St. Hallvard. B. 19. pp. 49–88.

1942 *The Papermaker* (U.S.A.). 'Wallpaper', No. 2, pp. 12–14.

1943 E. A. ENTWISLE. *The Connoisseur* (September). 'Eighteenth Century Decorators' and Paperhangers' Bills'. Illustrated.

1943 A. S. G. BUTLER, *Recording Ruin*, p. 139.

> *One thing is remarkable in the mêlée of bad detail and trashy decoration that I find. It is the triumph of Lincrusta. I do not mean aesthetically but quite the opposite, in a military sense. No material I think has stood up to blast so stoutly. That bumpy, adhesive skin on walls and ceilings, aping rich plasterwork, has counteracted many blows from bombs, even sustaining whole surfaces by itself. . . . It quite hurts me to think that something we have scoffed at for years has turned out a valuable ally in a fight. A pity it is so unattractive, especially when painted chocolate.*

1944 SHERRIL WHITON (Director, New York School of Interior Decoration), 'Elements of Interior Decoration' (1st edn. 1937, 2nd edn. Revised and Enlarged). Contains Chapter on Wallpaper, probably written by Miss Nancy McClelland. Illustrated.

1944 JOHN GLOAG, *The Englishman's Castle*. Illustrated by Marjorie Whittington, 2nd Edn, 1945; 3rd Edn., 1949. Interesting references to Wallpaper.

1945 Catalogue of the Exhibition of Historical and Modern Wallpapers held at Suffolk Galleries, London. Opened May 8, 1945. Introduction by Sacheverell Sitwell. Published by the Central Institute of Art and Design. Cover by Laurence Scarfe. Illustrated. Also 'Bibliography' of Wallpaper by E. A. Entwisle. (Supplement.)

(Many articles and critiques were written about this Exhibition which was the first major industrial exhibition to be put on in this country after the war, and may be said to have marked the beginning of public interest and discernment in matters of wallpaper design and colour.) Organised by T. A. FENNEMORE.

1945 *Punch*, apropos the Wallpaper Exhibition.

1,000 patterns of wallpaper are available for post-war use, and it is understood that the walls will follow.

1945 E. A. ENTWISLE. *The Connoisseur* (March). 'Historians of Wallpaper'. Of special interest from the bibliographical point of view.

1945 E. A. ENTWISLE. *Journal of Decorative Art* (January). 'A Pioneer of Wallpaper—Walmsley Preston of Darwen'. Walmsley Preston was prominently associated with the discovery of the wallpaper printing machine.

1945 JAMES LAVER. *The Lady* (March). 'Wallpapers'.

1945 *Vogue* (May). Short critique by CECIL BEATON.

It was only in the house of the very poor or of the artist that you would find a paper whose taste was not spoilt by respectability.

1945 *Building* (April). Critical article on wallpaper by MYERSCOUGH.

1945 *British Industries* (Journal of the Federation of British Industries) (October), 'English Wallpapers'.

1945 *British Standard* (*Wallpapers*) *1248*. Issued by British Standards Institution, 28 Victoria St., London, S.W.1. Revised 1954. [See below].

1945 *Walls and Wallpaper*. A Lecture given in May this year by JAMES LAVER at the National Gallery.

1945 *New Statesman* (May 26). Article entitled 'Design in The Home', written by ROGER MARVELL on the Wallpaper Exhibition, mentioned above.

1945 EVELYN WAUGH, *Brideshead Revisited* (Chapman & Hall). Describing one of the rooms:

. . . It was a charming room, oddly shaped to conform with the curve of the dome. The walls were papered in a pattern of ribbon and roses.

1945 LEATHER HANGINGS. J. W. WATERER, *Leather in Life, Art and Industry* (Faber & Faber, London). See also 1937, HANS HUTH; and 1950 Catalogue of Kassel Museum; HENRI CLOUZOT, *Cuirs Dorées, etc.*

1946 NANCY MCCLELLAND (in a speech about this time):

I often think when I see papered rooms that many people put it on very much as they put butter on bread. Here is the bread, here is the knife and here is the butter—now spread it from end to end of the wall! What a pity, when there are dozens of interesting ways in which wallpaper can be used —all of which enhance the value of the paper and the decorative mood it creates. . . . No other minor art has done so much to beautify our homes at so small an expense.

1946 E. R. YARHAM. *Britannia and Eve*, 'Wallpapers once were nailed'.

1947 ADA K. LONGFIELD, M.A. (Mrs. H. G. Leask) (December), 'History of the Dublin Wallpaper Industry in the 18th century'. Published in the *Journal of the Royal Society of Antiquaries of Ireland*, Vol. LXXVII, Part 2. [See further papers below].

1947 SIR AMBROSE HEAL, *Signboards of Old London Shops* (Batsford). See notes on old paperstaining businesses and their signs, pp. 143–4, etc.

1947 *Cyclopaedia of Decorating*, edited by W. P. MATTHEWS (2 Vols.). Contains section on paperhanging.

1947 *Cabinet Maker and Complete House Furnisher* (December 20). 'A Christmas of the Past.' Reference to an Exhibition by Wm. Woollams Ltd. at Earls Court in 1897.

1947 H. LASSEN, *Tapetets Historie* (Faaborg).

1947 *Apollo* (November). Short article on Chinese Wallpapers.

1947 CHARLES MORGAN, *The Judge's Story*, concerning a house at 'Champion Road', Cliftonville, where the judge retires to write his *magnum opus.*

> *Only above the bed, the mantelpiece, and the chest of drawers did wallpaper appear—a design of blue barges, trees, canals and windmills on a buff ground.* Again: . . . *I thought you would like to hang this* (*a pastel by Sickert*) *for yourself. The wallpaper's pretty grim.*

1947 PAMELA HANSFORD JOHNSON, *An Avenue of Stone*, Part 3, Chapter 1. Mrs. Olney, owner of a Kensington bric-à-brac shop says:

> '*I'll make lampshades out of customers' own materials . . . you know, to match their rooms . . . or even walls if there was a patterned paper, only you don't often see patterned papers. Which I think is a pity,' Field interpolated, 'Wallpapers can be quite smashing if they're well designed. I'm getting as sick of creams and off-whites as people got of the beiges and oatmeals of the twenties.*'

1948 DR. NICKOLAUS PEVSNER, *Design in Relation to Industry through the Ages.* Read before The Royal Society of Arts (November 24). References to Réveillon, Oberkampf, William Morris, Metford Warner, etc.

1948 *The Masque.* Editor, LIONEL CARTER. (Curtain Press, London). Rex Whistler drawings for stage settings. The Nursery (Old Music) Act 1, Scene 1; (Streamline); (A Place of one's Own); etc. [See plate No. 84].

1948 ADA K. LONGFIELD, M.A. (Mrs. H. G. Leask), 'The Manufacture of Raised Stucco or Papier Maché Papers in Ireland, *c.* 1750–1770, and 'Old Wallpapers in Ireland'. Both articles published in *The Journal of the Royal Society of Antiquaries in Ireland*, Vol. LXXVIII, Part 1 (July) and Part II (December) respectively.

1948 CLIFFORD MUSGRAVE, *The Royal Pavilion.* (Director of Brighton Art Gallery and Museum). 39 pages. 4 plates. Contains interesting references to Chinese wallpapers and the decorating work by Crace & Sons, in the Royal Pavilion, Brighton, p. 15. (*Continued on page 179*)

112 Visit of H.M. Queen Elizabeth the Queen Mother to Suffolk Galleries, Suffolk Street, London S.W.1, on the occasion of the Exhibition of Historical and British Wallpapers, May 1945

113 Hand printed wallpaper 'Quatrefoil' designed by Edward Bawden for Cole & Son (Wallpapers) Ltd, *c.*1950

The three persons chiefly responsible for the decorative work in the Pavilion, Frederick Crace, Lambelet and Robert Jones, are unknown except for their work here.

[See above, 1939 Monograph on J. G. Crace].

1948 RALPH DUTTON, *The English Interior* (Batsford). See references to wallpaper, pp. 126–9, 144, 169, etc.

English wallpaper manufacturers of the mid-19th century considered themselves pre-eminent in Europe in their art: thus, as was to be expected, the Great Exhibition contained a liberal supply of their products. In the Mediaeval Court were to be seen four of Pugin's designs for papers to be used in the Houses of Parliament. . . . Other exhibits designed for less august precincts struck a brighter and more frivolous note, but the majority were so dominant in colour and pattern that their effect would have been crushing in any room in which they were hung.

1948 MARGARET JOURDAIN. *Country Life* (October 1). *Chinese Paperhangings.* Illustrated.

A writer in The World *speaking of Chinese papers describes the rooms of a house which were formerly wainscoted, as hung with the richest China and India paper, where all the flowers of fancy are exhausted in a thousand fantastic figures of birds, beasts and fishes which never had existence.*

1948 ERIC GILL, *Letters of Eric Gill*, edited by Walter Shewring (apropos hand versus machine-made goods).

Now here's my trouble. I don't believe the human race is capable of such a sacrifice. I believe it will still demand wallpapers and muck of that sort, and patterns on biscuit boxes.

1948 H. J. HITCH, 'Wallpapers', *Architectural Review* (November). An informed article on the development of wallpaper design in Scandinavia, with special reference to Danish successes. The author states that there is no reason why wallpaper should be confined to domestic interiors as it is a useful medium for institutional buildings, an aspect 'quite neglected in England.'

1948 ALLEN W. SEABY, *Pattern without Pain* (Batsford). A practical and interesting instructional book on general designing.

1948 *Nation Belge* (February 28). Special Supplement dealing with wallpaper, including an interesting article on the Dominotiers.

The etymology of the words 'dominoes' 'dominoterie' was being discussed. Perhaps they originated from the fact that the most ancient wood-cuts depicted the Lord Christ (Dominus) or from the fact that gaudy coloured papers, so called wrappers, used to cover objects such as boxes, books, etc., like a coloured garment—a domino. Until the end of the 16th century all wood-engravers were known as 'dominotiers'. Then they called all papers printed in black and coloured by stencil 'dominoteries' or 'dominos'. The Royal Declaration of November, 1640, gives this definition: 'Dominoterie, otherwise stained paper. . . .'

1949 E. A. ENTWISLE, *English Wallpaper Design from the 18th Century to the Present Day*. Read to the British Colour Council's Designers' Course (April 27). [See Reports in *The Decorator*, *The Builder* (May), etc].

The post-war picture of wallpaper design was not yet sufficiently stable or clear, but the lecturer believed that design and pattern were coming back into their own and that colour was better appreciated than before.

1949 A. E. HURST. *Painting and Decorating*. See Chapter 30, 'Wallpaper and other Hangings', includes interesting references to Varieties, Dimensions, Selection of, etc.; and Chapter 31, 'Paperhanging'. (Griffin, London.) Illustrated. A reliable reference book on the subject.

1949 WALTER STENGEL, *Tapeten*, Markisches Museum, Berlin.

1949 *Paper and Print*, 'The History of Wallpaper'. Illustrated. Vol. 22, No. 1.

1949 SIR AMBROSE HEAL. *Country Life* (July 22). *Paperstainers of the 17th and 18th Centuries*. (Reference principally to Trade Cards.) Illustrated.

1949 NIKOLAUS PEVSNER, *The Listener, March 17*. 'From William Morris to Walter Gropius' (the first of three talks on the Third Programme, on the Bauhaus). A useful contribution to the history of industrial design.

1949 *Country Life Annual*. Articles on nineteenth-century French wallpaper and one by GRACE LOVAT FRASER reviewing wallpaper over the past half-century.

1949 *World's Paper Trade Review* (May 19). Account of a Wallpaper Exhibition held at the Colour, Design and Style Centre, Manchester, and opened by Mr. S. Gordon Russell, C.B.E. (now Sir Gordon Russell).

1949 SARTRE, *Intimacy* (Peter Nevill Ltd.). A collection of short stories translated from the French by Lloyd Alexander. One of these, entitled 'The Room', contains the following reference. '. . . *Threats were written on the wall, Eve knew it but she could not read them. She often watched the big red roses on the wallpaper until they began to dance before her eyes. The roses flamed in shadow . . . there were also white discs on the wall that looked like slices of onion. The discs spun and Eve's hands began to tremble. . . .*'

1949 ARNE BJÖNNES,' Vallo Wallpaper Factory and the Norwegian Sandpaper Factory'. Byggekunst. *Building Art*, p. 182.

1950 AUGUST DERLETH. *Weird Tales* (U.S.A.), Vol. 42, No. 6, September. 'Potts' Triumph'. A highly imaginative story of an arrogant interior decorator, Philander Potts, who undertakes to redecorate a room of an old house occupied many years ago by two old and eccentric spinsters. Their old French wallpaper resists removal, but when at last the new one, put up by Potts, is in position, the decorator has disappeared and his small figure is from then on only to be seen, by those who have eyes to see, imprisoned in the pattern of the new figured wallpaper.

1950 Council of Industrial Design. A Design Folio, *Wallpaper for the Small Home* (contains actual samples). This folio was prepared by STELLA CARLISLE.

Reaction came in the 1920's. People had suffered a surfeit of pattern, and even of colour, and they turned to plainness and washed their walls in

(*Continued on page 185*)

114 A machine printed wallpaper designed by Lucienne Day, 1954

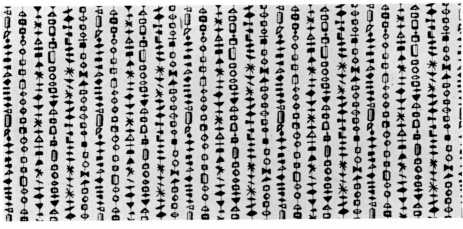

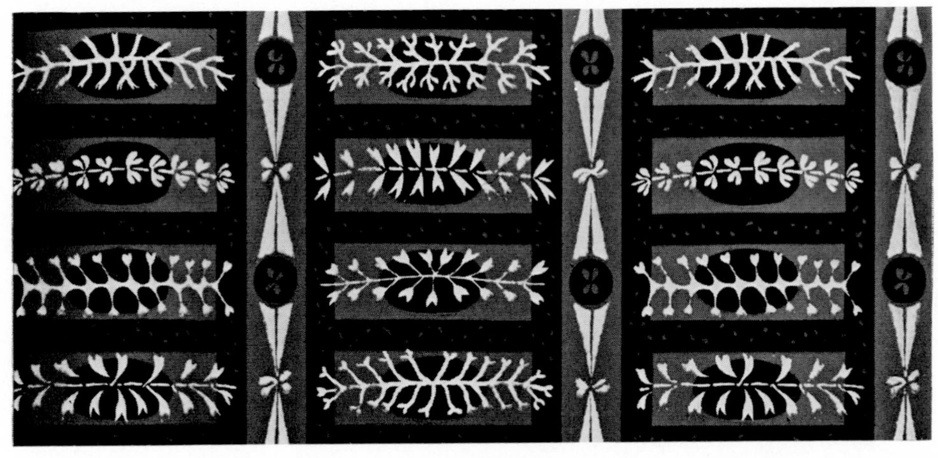

115 Two colourings of a design for a machine printed wallpaper by Robert Nicholson, 1958, both produced by The Wall Paper Manufacturers Ltd

116 A machine printed wallpaper produced by The Wall Paper Manufacturers Ltd, 1958

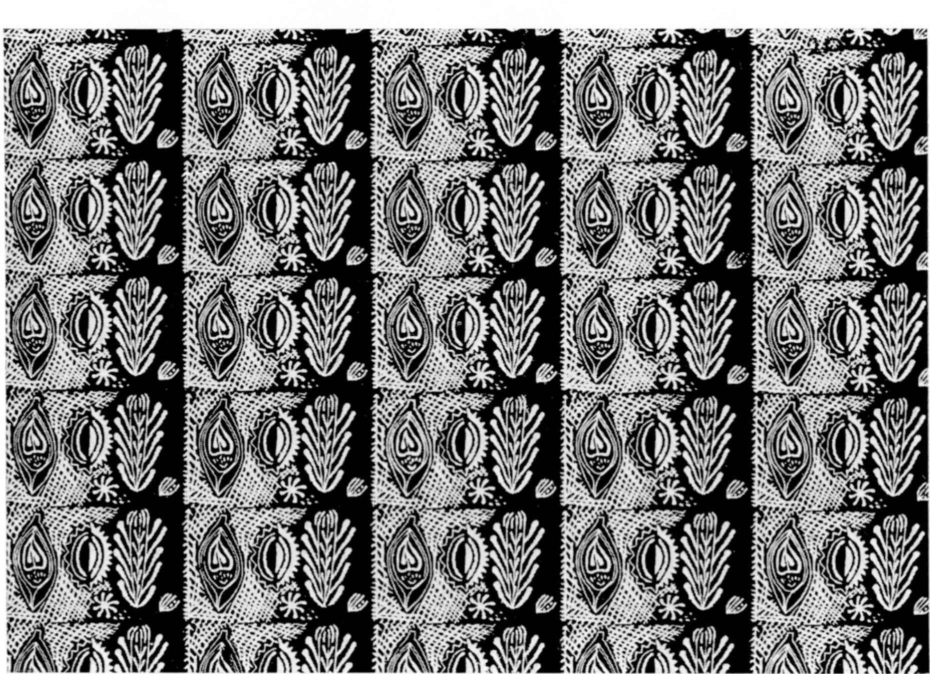

117 A screen printed design produced by Hayward & Son Ltd, 1955

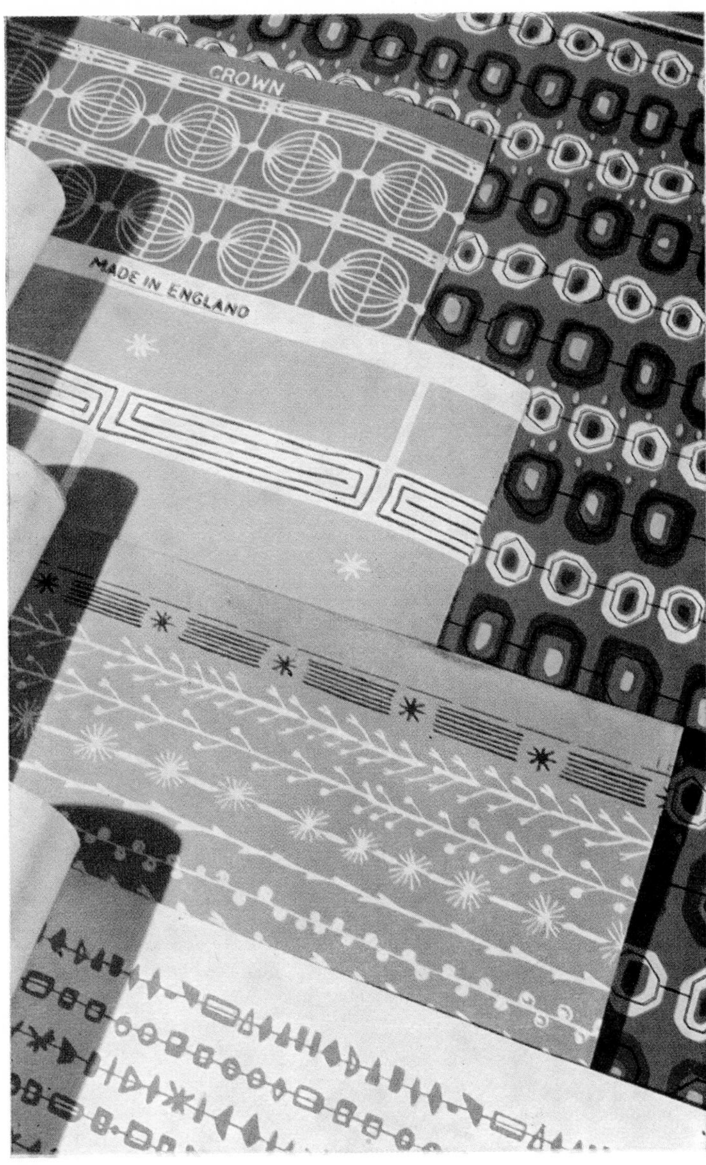

118 A selection of inexpensive machine-printed English wallpapers of the 1954 period, typifying the new and growing emphasis on simple pattern and imaginative colour

off white colours. It was the only time in the history of English interiors when walls were plain by choice, and the most popular wallpapers were those that denied their patterned ancestry and dwindled into an indeterminate blur. Now, wallpaper is finding its way back to livelier pattern and colours, and everyone who buys wallpaper plays some part in deciding whether this tendency will develop, and if so, whether it will develop on good lines or bad.

1950 ADA K. LONGFIELD, M.A. (Mrs. H. G. Leask), 'Old Wallpapers and Wall Paintings in Ireland', published in *The Journal of the Royal Society of Antiquaries in Ireland*, Vol. LXXX, Part 2.

1950 MARGARET JOURDAIN, *English Interior Decoration, 1500-1830* (Batsford). A Study in the Development of Design. Pp. 78, Plates 195, Index, Notes, etc.

1950 MOSCHER, *Specialty Papers* (U.S.A.). Contains chapter on Wallpaper, its history, manufacture, etc.

1950 *Chambers's Encyclopaedia.* Article on Wallpaper by MARGARET JOURDAIN, with special reference to the French contribution to the development of the industry.

1950 E. A. ENTWISLE. *The Connoisseur* (May). 'The Blew Paper Warehouse in Aldermanbury'. Detailed notes on the progress of this wallpaper-making firm from 1700 to Victorian times.

1950 R. BROOKE-CAWS, *Notes on the Origin and History of Coutts & Company.* Brief reference to the famous Chinese wallpaper presented to the Bank by Lord Macartney in 1794.

1950 *The Bowater Papers*, No. 1. A magazine issued (May) by the Bowater Paper Corporation, containing, on p. 49, an article illustrated in colour entitled 'Walls have Souls Too'—a potted history of the subject.

Among the pleasant things in life which the return of peacetime plenty will bring us is the supply of wallpaper in new and traditional designs. The wall austere and colour washed, or covered with tired and fading paper, has been with us too long.

1950 *Indoors* (July). The Trust House Review. 'A Hundred Years of History on the Wall.'

1950 JOHN PRINCE LOWENSTEIN. *Everybody's* (November 18). 'Within Four Walls'. Illustrated.

1950 *Sanderson Commentary.* A quarterly House Organ, commenced September, and still running.

1950 F. RULLMANN, *Die Tapete* (Stuttgart).

1950 *Führer Durch das Deutsches Tapeten-Museum un Weissensteinflügel des Schlosse-Wilhelmshöehe.* Catalogue of the Famous Wallpaper Museum at Kassel. Illustrated. Written by PROFESSOR FR. MACHMAR.

Extract from the Preface: '*The German Wallpaper Museum, the only institution of its kind in the world, is a trade museum of the German*

Wallpaper Manufacturers' Association. In sixteen rooms of the Weissen Steinflügel of the Wilhelmshöhe Palace at Kassel a collection of valuable wallpapers of all kinds, ages and origins demonstrating the history of civilization in this field, is exhibited.'

1950 FRANCES LICHTEN, *Decorative Art of Victoria's Era.* (Chas. Scribner, New York). Illustrated. References to wallpaper. Bibliography, etc.

. . . these sombre mid-Victorian mantel (pieces) were set off by wallpapers whose heavy luscious tones conveyed the suggestion of plum-pudding fruitiness then thought highly desirable. When walls were not covered with gilt rococo scrollings or with highly naturalistic representations of flowers and fruit, the house keeper was apt to choose a conventional design in self-colour, the texture of which bore a close resemblance to the skin of a peach. . . .

In the 1840's and 1850's self-toned rococo, floral or landscape designs, in neutral colours (gray, stone, pearl), were in the best style. To give a finish to these quiet hues one could purchase blocked borderings . . . favourite border motifs were festoons of drapery, richly fringed and caught, at intervals with clusters of flowers. . . .

1951 LOIS and WILLIAM KATZENBACH. *Practical Book of American Wallpapers* (Lippincott, U.S.A.). Illustrated. Including 12 specimens.

1951 The Wall Paper Manufacturers Ltd *The Pattern of a Great Organization.* A Jubilee Publication. Profusely illustrated. Privately printed.

1951 ADA K. LONGFIELD (Mrs. H. G. Leask), 'Old Wallpapers in Ireland'. Published in *The Journal of the Royal Society of Antiquaries of Ireland,* Vol. LXXXI, Part 2.

1951 *Design in the Festival,* published by The Council of Industrial Design (May). On p. 27 wallpapers illustrated in colour.

1951 Royal Society of Arts. 'Exhibition of Exhibitions.' Reported in *The Architect's Journal* (August 16). Wallpaper represented.

1951 E. A. ENTWISLE. *Architectural Review* (December). 'An Eighteenth-Century Flock Wallpaper'. Illustrated. Refers to the Flock Wallpaper, 'Les deux pigeons', at Clandon Park, near Guildford. See also illustrated article in *Surrey Archaeological Collections,* Vol. LII (1952).

1951 *Design* (No. 36). Article by 'C.D.', 'Limited Editions'. A review of a new collection of screen-printed wallpapers issued by John Line & Sons Ltd., London.

1951 *Church of England Newspaper and Record* (March 30).

In my grandmother's house when I was a child there was a little bedroom papered specially for me in a pattern of pink sweet peas tied up with blue ribbon bows. I used to lie in bed marvelling that human hands could have made anything so pretty.

1951 KATHARINE MORRISON MCCLINTON, *Antique Collecting for Everyone* (U.S.A.). In 1952 abridgement of *Antique Collecting.* See article, 'American Wallpapers'. Mostly relating to bandbox papers. [See 1952].

119 Three Centuries of Taste and Comment. A 'literary' exhibition of wallpapers arranged by the author at Foyle's Art Gallery, Charing Cross Road, 1–25 Feb., 1956

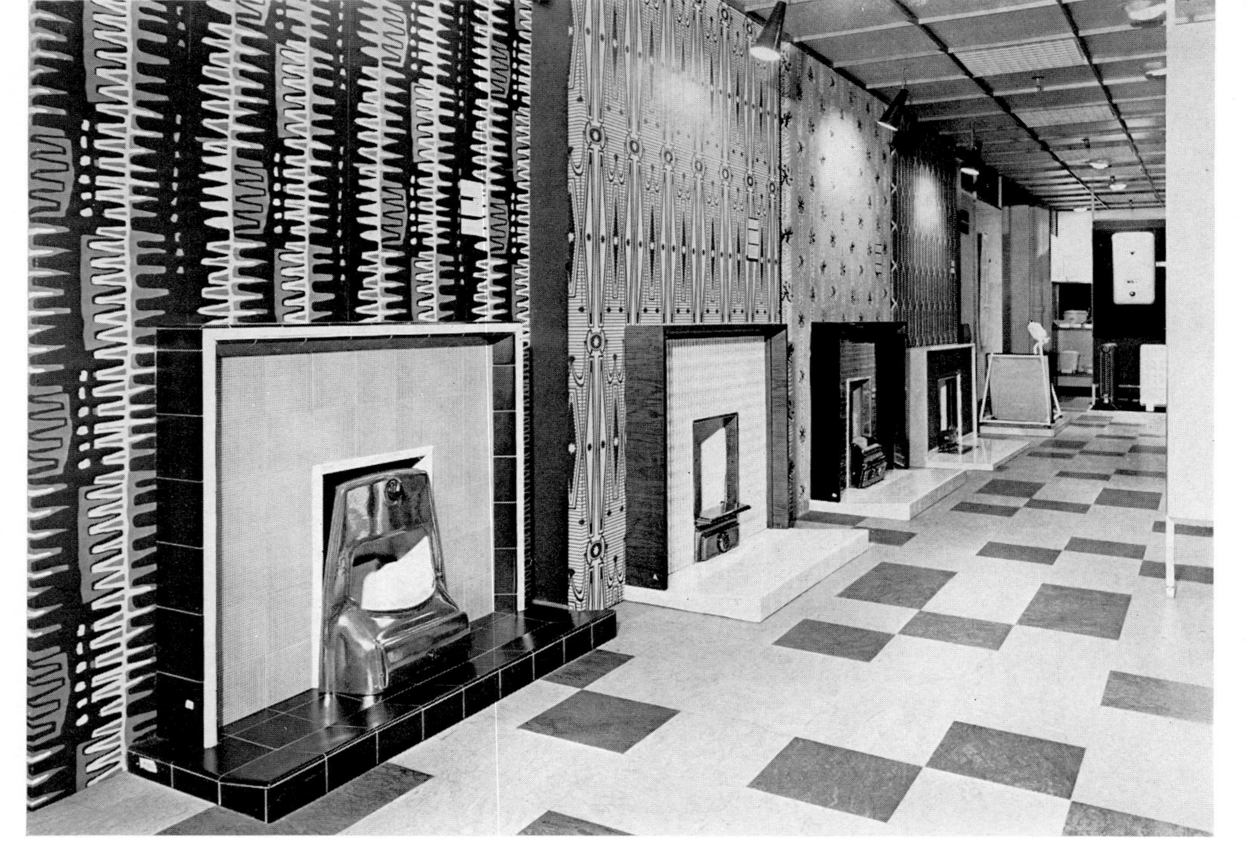

120 First display of wallpaper at The Design Centre, Haymarket, S.W.1., 1956, showing, from left to right, hand printed wallpapers produced by Palladio, Coles and Sandersons

1952 M. EDWARD INGRAM, *Leaves from a Family Tree*. The story of the Grimston family of Yorkshire, and the building of Kilnwick Manor. Mentions Bromwich and other eighteenth-century paper-stainers.

1952 IRIS BROOKE, *Four Walls Adorned*. (Methuen.) Illustrated. A useful reference book on English interior decoration, from 1485-1820.

1952 PAPERMAKING. A monumental reference book on this subject. E. J. LABARRE. *Dictionary and Encyclopaedia of Paper and Paper Making*. (Swets & Zeitlinger, Amsterdam). 500 pages. Illustrated. 2nd edition. Contains an article on wallpaper as well as special articles on Marble papers, Philately, Water-marks, etc.

> *The term 'wallpaper manufacturer' is more frequently encountered to-day than the old style 'paperhanging maker' or 'paper-stainer', the latter to describe one who stained or coloured paper.'*

[See also R. H. Clapperton, Dard Hunter and other authorities on the history of papermaking.]

1952 AYLMER VALLANCE. *New Statesman and Nation* (August 6). 'Tapestry and Images'.

> *For instance, in Mortimer Street, not far from the Hare's Foot, patronised by the gold beaters, is a rambling Georgian shop, somewhat overshadowed by Medicine Monumental in the shape of the Middlesex Hospital. It is the trading outpost of a factory—workroom, atelier, call it what you will—deep in the modest obscurity of Islington but carrying on the true tradition of the 'dominotiers, tapissiers et imagiers' who formed a guild in 1586 for the production of marbled, damasked, and pictured papers for hanging* on domestic walls. . . . A literary effusion.

1952 D. DEWAR MILLS. *Architectural Review* (October), 'Wallpapers'. Critical article on wallpaper design. (Illustrated).

> . . . *But although much has been done to improve the quality and variety of mass produced wallpapers there again appears a reluctance to give modern design a free hand. . . . It is time for the manufacturers to pass a vote of confidence on to the designers who can then forsake the safety of their stripes, classical medallions, and timid small scale textures and work within wider terms of reference more closely tuned to modern trends of design.*

1952 *Times Commercial* (April 10).

> *Vigorous colour is not allowed to overwhelm the modern room. It is wisely restricted to two or three areas and applied with skill and purpose. Striking wallpaper when confined to one wall is more effective than if used on the four.*

1952 ROGER SMITHELLS. *Model Housekeeping* (January). 'The House Beautiful'.

> *I must issue a solemn warning against some of the terrible things that can be done with wallpaper in the name of decoration. Some wallpaper manufacturers have produced the most deplorable collections of ornamental strips, floral cut-outs, medallions, birds, butterflies, galleons, and so forth, intended to be applied as friezes, borders, elaborate and meaningless panels and scenic effects. Once you have started to stick these things on*

to your walls the process is liable to go to your head. The urge to fill a blank space with just one more clump of delphiniums or a couple of humming birds may finally land you with a complete herbaceous border, a teeming jungle, or a perpetual view of the whole of the Spanish Armada in full sail.

1952 *Antique Collecting*. Fawcett Publications, Greenwich, Connecticut. Edited by KATHARINE MORRISON MCCLINTON. This journal deals mainly with the use of wallpaper as band-box covers. See article 'American Wallpapers'.

Early American wallpapers and wallpaper-covered bandboxes, particularly those with historical scenes, offer an interesting and comparatively inexpensive field for the antique collector, and for the researcher too. Up to now few exact data have been uncovered. Several writers have recorded the names of the first 'paperstainers' or wall paper manufacturers, but just which maker manufactured a certain pattern or at what date the pattern was first made is not often known. However wallpaper was made in considerable quantities in eighteenth-century America, and there were early makers in Philadelphia, Boston, New York as well as in a few other towns. Plunket Fleeson of Philadelphia is credited with making the first wallpaper in America in 1739.

1952 E. GIANNI, 'Le Tappezzerie di Carta' in the Italian Journal *Rivista di Ingegneria*, No. 6 (June), General Description of the Manufacture of Wallpaper in Italy.

1952 DECORATED PAPERS. R. B. LORING, *Decorated Book Papers* (Harvard University Press, 1st Edn., 1942). Demonstrates the link between this craft and paper-staining.

1952 E. A. ENTWISLE. *The Connoisseur* (October). Eighteenth-century London Paperstainers. Thomas Bromwich at the Golden Lyon on Ludgate Hill. Illustrated. Continuing the series on old wallpaper makers.

1952 *Catalogue of an Exhibition of Victorian and Edwardian Decorative Arts.* At Victoria and Albert Museum. H.M.S.O. Introduction by PETER FLOUD. An indispensable source book on the designers of the periods named. This very successful exhibition included many examples of wallpaper by such designers as: A. W. N. Pugin; Owen Jones; Bruce J. Talbert; Christopher Dresser; Charles L. Eastlake; William Morris; William Burges; E. W. Godwin; Lewis F. Day; Walter Crane; Heywood Sumner; Jessie M. King; C. F. A. Voysey, etc.

1952 LUISA HAGER, *Alte Wandbespannungen und Tapeten* (Darmstadt). Illustrated.

1953 *Specifications for Wallpaper*. Issued by The Wall Paper Manufacturers Ltd. A reference book for the Architect, Decorator and Display Consultant. Layout by CHARLES HASLER.

1953 B. H. HELLMANN, 'The Story of Wallpaper'. Reprinted from the American periodical *The Wallpaper Magazine*.

1953 ALEXANDER KOCH, *Dekorationsstoffe Tapeten/Teppiche* (Stuttgart). Copiously illustrated and containing actual samples of wallpaper made by European firms.

121 A display of wallpaper at Olympia, London, 1957

122 A typical wallpaper printing machine showing colour boxes being replenished

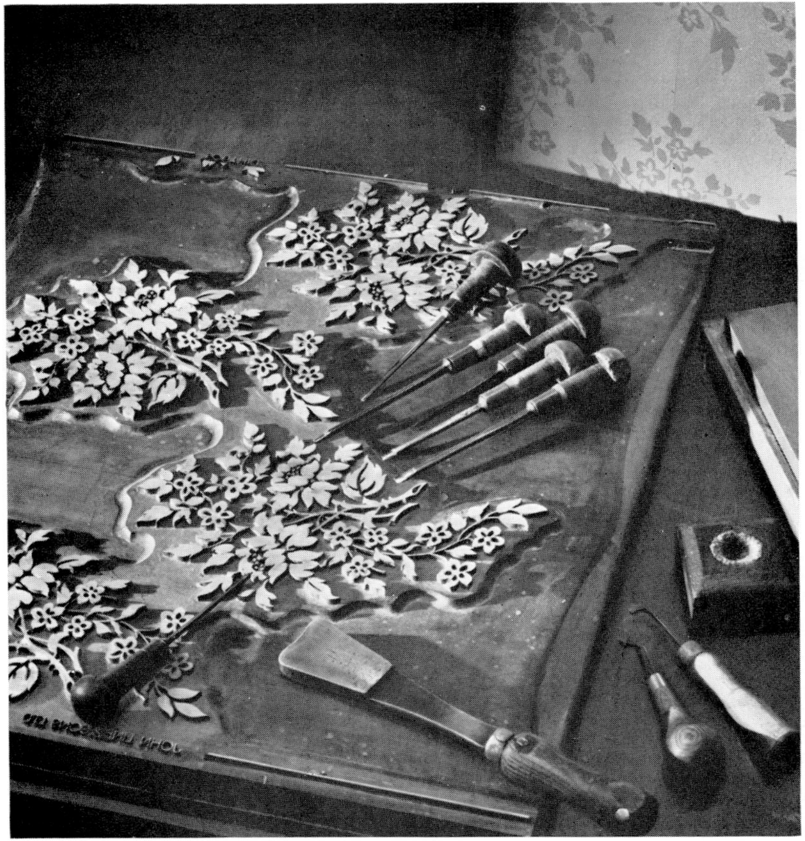

123 A finished printing block showing block cutters' tools (John Line & Sons Ltd)

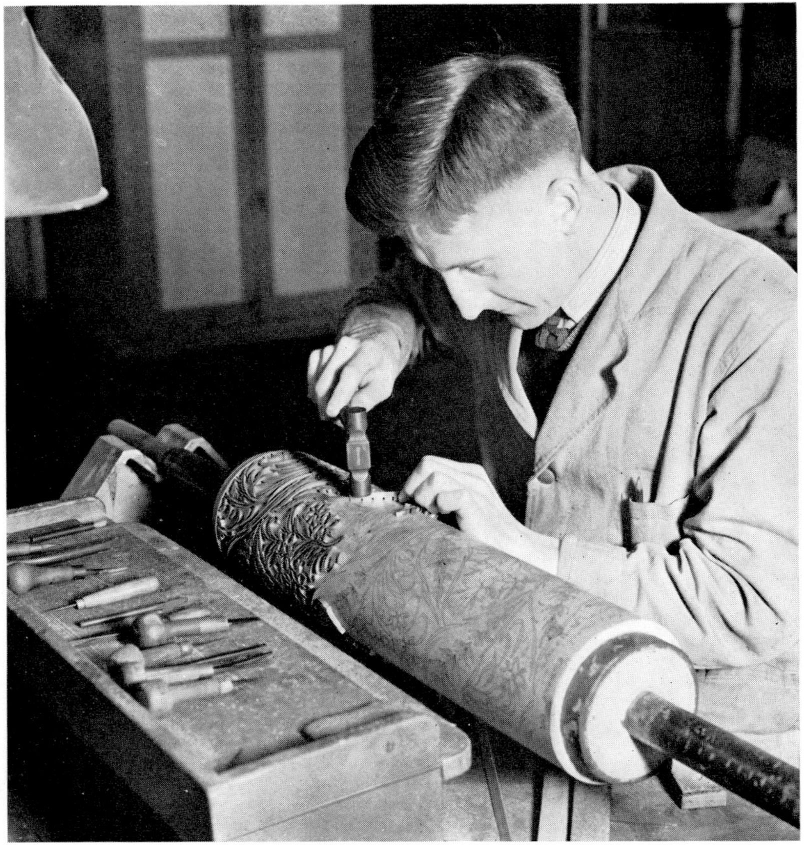

124 Roller cutter at work on the preparation of a surface roller (John Line & Sons Ltd)

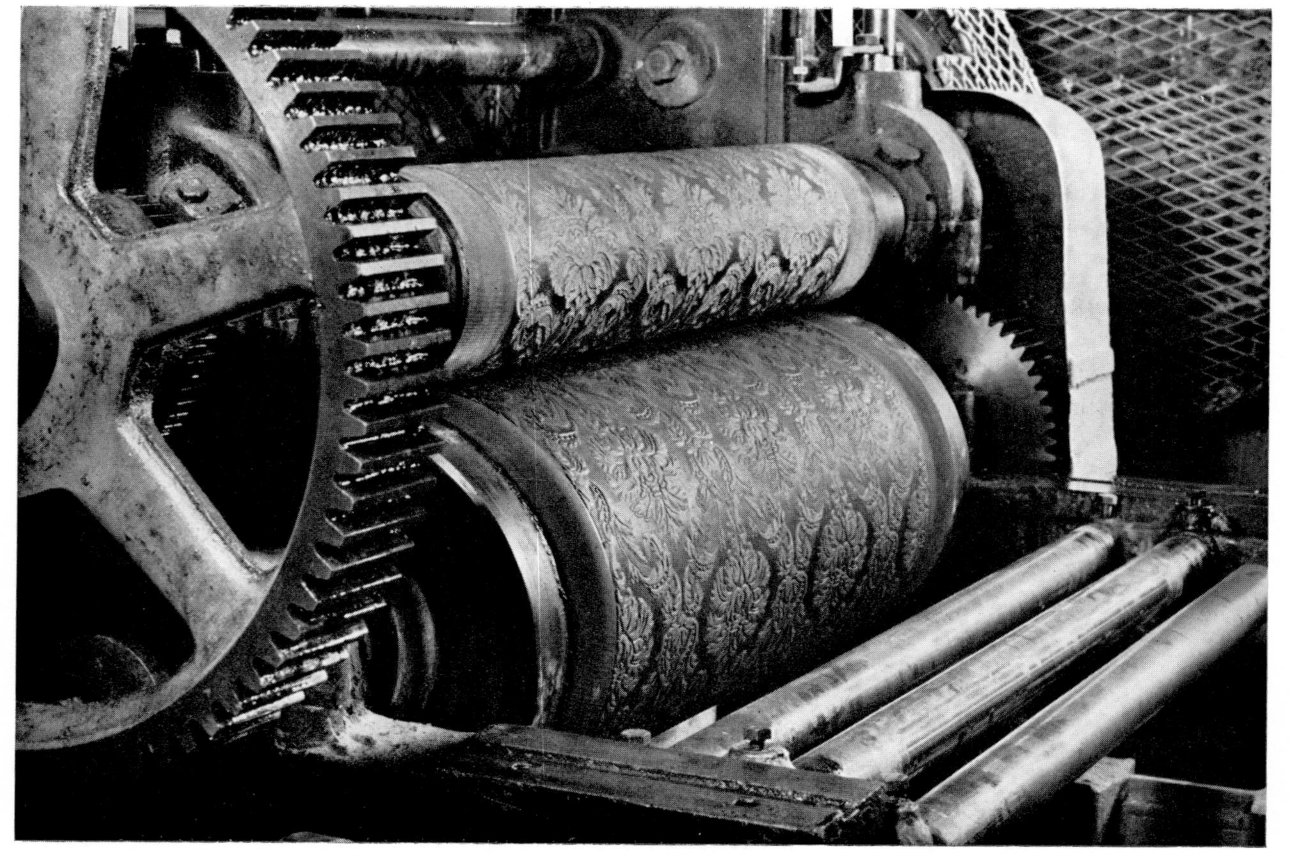

125 Machine used in the production of embossed wallpaper

1953 *The Decorator* (January). 'Wallpaper 1837-1910—Victoria and Albert Centenary Exhibition'.

1953 A. JACKSON. *Financial Times* (Paper and Board Supplement), November 16. Useful article on the wallpaper industry.

1953 E. A. ENTWISLE. *The Decorator* (August). 'The German Wallpaper Museum, Kassel'.

1953 E. A. ENTWISLE. *Country Life* (July 16). 'Early Wallpapers'. Reference to the discovery at Gwernhaylod, Flintshire, of one of the oldest wallpapers to be found *in situ* in this country. Illustrated.

1953 *The Lady* (September 3).

The Productivity Council recommends that shoe manufacturers should reduce costs and use fewer designs . . . and indeed, the lay person may well wonder what deep trade secret can be behind the multiplicity of indecisive patterns, in porridge or roast chicken shades which is so depressing to search through when a wallpaper has to be chosen.

1953 CONSTANCE DE PINNA. *I.C.I. Magazine* (November). 'Wallpapers'.

Wallpaper is like gunpowder, if you are too timid with it the effect is unsettling; if you overdo it the result can be devastating.

1953 PAUL REILLY. *Design* (July). Article on 'German Enterprise in Wallpaper Design'.

1953 (July). Exhibition of Wallpapers, Musée Galliera, Paris. Extract from roneoed 'hand out' includes a brief history of Wallpaper.

Cette exposition a été organisée par la Société des Décorateurs Français en collaboration avec les fabricants de papiers peints français, membres de la Chambre Syndicale des Papiers Peints de France. Son but est de montrer au public l'intérêt d'un materiaux d'origine française qui a toujours été a l'honneur dans les decorations murales.

1953 *House & Garden's New Complete Guide to Interior Decoration* (Simon & Schuster, New York). Contains many references to wallpaper.

1953 The Return of Wallpaper? A Luncheon Meeting arranged by the Design and Industries Association at the Royal Society, Burlington House (January 5). Speakers: D. Dewar Mills and E. A. Entwisle. Reported in the *Cabinetmaker*, January 9.

1953 *Design* (June). Article by 'J.E.B.', 'New Patterns on Paper'.

1953 *Georgian Wallpapers* (I). Paper read to the York Georgian Society. E. A. ENTWISLE (January 23). Reported in the Society Year Book [See 1955.]

1954 E. A. ENTWISLE, *The Book of Wallpaper*. A History and an Appreciation. Introduction by Sacheverell Sitwell. 150 pp. 72 half-tone illustrations, 3 in colour. Quarto. (Arthur Barker, London).

Extract from SACHEVERELL SITWELL'S Introduction: *Visions on paper which tatter and fade, but are not transitory.*

1954 *Wallpaper Design and Craftsmanship*. Paper read to The Art Workers' Guild, 8 Queen's Square, W.C.1 (April 23), by E. A. ENTWISLE.

1954 *Daily Herald*, 'The Buying Habits and Purchasing Power of this newspaper's Readers'. Painting and Decorating Section (May). Statistics are given showing percentages of wallpaper and paint used by readers.

1954 British Standards Institution *Wallpapers*. British Standard Specification 1248/1954. 23 pp.

Special reference should be made to the length of 11½ yd.; as it is understood that some users assume that a roll of wallpaper should measure 12 yd. Before wallpaper was made in continuous lengths a 'piece' was generally composed of twelve sheets of paper pasted together end to end. These 'pieces' were known as 'dozens' and it was popularly assumed that they contained a dozen yards. In fact each separate sheet measured approximately 22 in. × 35 in., thus making a total length of about 11½ yd. and this became the accepted length for a roll.

1954 *Times Review of Industry* (September), 'Wallpaper regains its Popularity', from a correspondent.

Almost 70% of all the wallpapers produced in the United Kingdom are now sold through retailers, who, broadly speaking, handle the cheaper end of the market, although today the higher priced papers are also to some extent sold across shop counters. The North West of England is generally recognised as the home of the wallpaper industry which has about twelve manufacturing plants in Lancashire, Cheshire and Yorkshire, but there are three mills in the Greater London area. The ten wallpaper mills, including the branch manufacturing relief decorations, of The Wall Paper Manufacturers Ltd. produce about 70% of the total output. The labour force of the industry (which is highly capitalized), at the manufacturing end, is approximately 5,000.

1954 W. MACQUEEN-POPE, *Back Numbers* (Hutchinson). 'A Cavalcade of Victoriana'. [See Wallpaper references under 1890].

1954 *The Book of Wallpaper* [See 1954 above.] A large number of reviews and critiques of this book appeared in various magazines and newspapers this year and in 1955-6. Notably in: *The Sunday Times* (October 17, 1954); *The Manchester Guardian* (November 19, 1954); *Times Literary Supplement* (November 20, 1954); *The Connoisseur* (December 1954); *Ambassador* (January 1955); *New Statesman and Nation* (January 22, 1955); *Apollo* (January 1955); *Time and Tide* (February 12, 1955); *Country Life* (February 24, 1955); *The Lady* (March 31, 1955); *Design* (May 1955); *Architectural Review* (August 1955); *Royal Society of Arts Journal* (September 16, 1955); *Burlington Magazine* (October 1956).

1954 *Punch* (March 3). From an article on the 'Contemporary Cult'.

But at least we are over the period of chronic distemper. Wallpapers are important again. It is accepted now that all the walls need not have the same treatment, that an individually papered alcove is not eccentric, that sometimes the most successful place to put a bold paper is on the ceiling. Designers can go the whole hog using colours which would be death if used on all four walls; black, brown and fern green backgrounds; purples, magentas. . . . But traditional designs of the late 18th and early

(*Continued on page 199*)

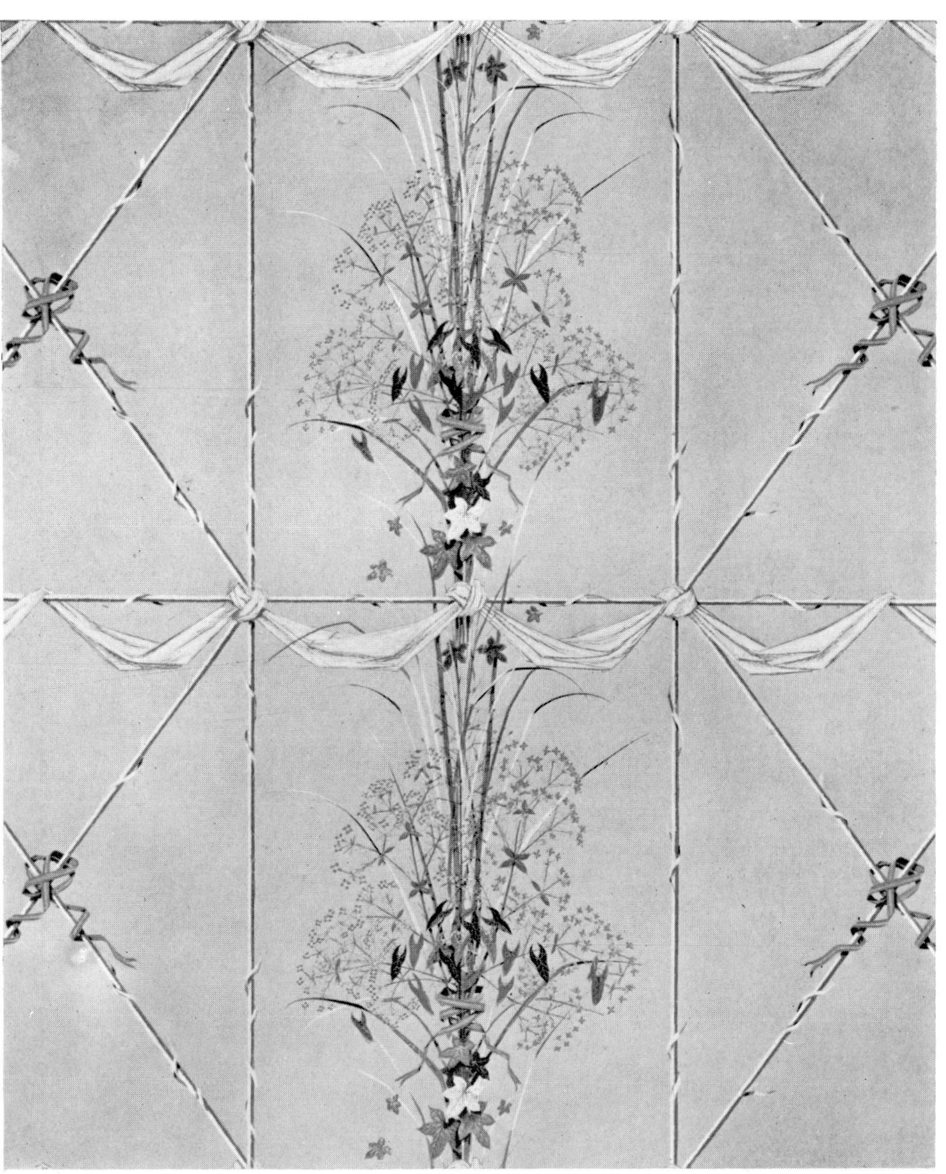

126 Wallpaper designed by Roger Nicholson and produced by The Wall Paper Manufacturers Ltd specially for the Caledonian Hotel, Edinburgh, 1959

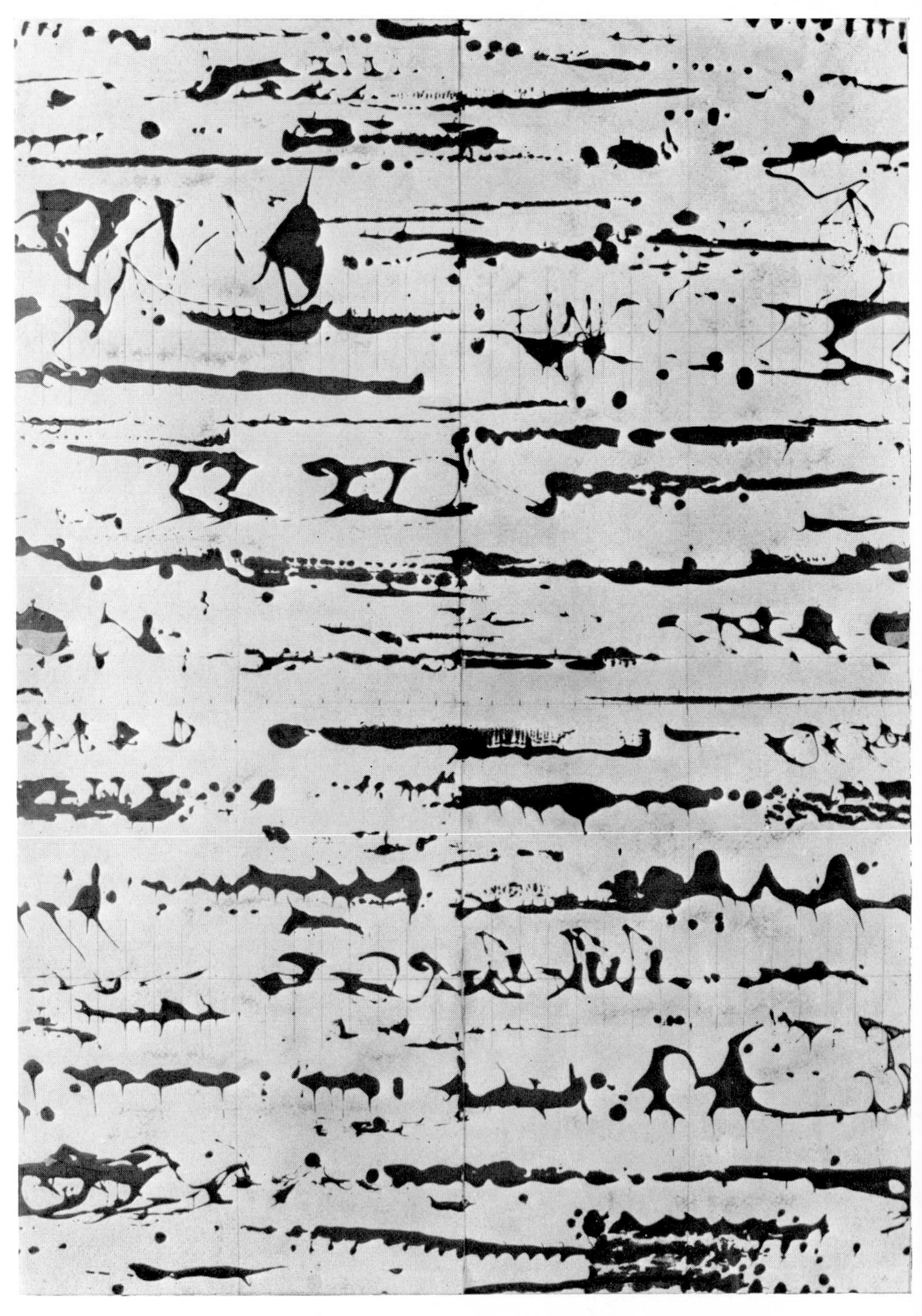

127 Design for wallpaper by William Gear commissioned by The Wall Paper Manufacturers Ltd, London, for their "Modus" collection, 1960

19th centuries reproduced in modern colours, are the best sellers. Among the traditionals there are many trellises, much ivy: and these papers tie up so conveniently with the contemporary HORTITECTURE *that many imagine they are, in fact, contemporary.*

1954 HILDA HUNTER. *The Antique Dealer and Collectors' Guide* (October) (London), 'Handmaiden of the Arts.' The story of wallpaper.

1954 DECORATED PAPERS. *Decorated Book Papers* (*Seventeenth to Twentieth Century*). Catalogue of an Exhibition at the Cooper Union Museum, New York. Mentions the *Dominotiers,* and includes a useful list of references to this subject.

1954 OTTO ULMSCHNEIDER, *Neuzeitliches Tapezieren Dekorieren, etc.* (Munchen). Illustrated. A practical book on various kinds of wallpaper in Germany and how to hang them.

1955 *Deutsches Tapeten Museum, Kassel.* New edition of the Catalogue of this Museum. [See 1950 above.]

1955 INGEMAR TUNANDER, *Tapeter.* Nordiska Museet, Stockholm. Extremely comprehensive book on the development of wallpaper in Sweden. Many unusual illustrations. (Bibliography).

1955 *Georgian Wallpapers* (II). Paper read to the York Georgian Society by E. A. ENTWISLE (January 25). Chairman, Mr. G. Howard.

1955 *Crystals and Wallpaper.* A Public Lecture given by PROFESSOR A. J. C. WILSON at University College, Cardiff (March 1).

1955 ROBERT SMUTZLER, *Architectural Review* (February). 'The English Origins of Art Nouveau'. p. 109.

1955 *The Times,* 4th Leader, 'Wallpaper' (September 19).

Few occupations can satisfy so swiftly and completely as papering a room can the human need to bring order out of mess, beauty out of little back bedrooms. The man with the brush and the step ladder has the feeling of creating a not contemptible work of art. It should live at least for a year or two, and if covered up then by layers of later work may come to a kind of concealed immortality, unsuspected until future generations, digging about in the ruins, discover his wallpaper and wonder how he did it.

1955 *Tapeten Zeitung* (March) Stuttgart; Interesting articles on the English Wallpaper Industry, Styles, Methods of Publicity, etc. (Illustrated).

1955 WILLIAM JUSTEMA. *Interiors* (October) (an American magazine). Article entitled 'Wallpapers and Painting'.

Pattern is wallpaper's chief reason for being. . . . Although wallpapers began as an imitation of costly materials they have long since established themselves as a decorative device unlike any other. Just as the charm of an Impressionist painting (and indeed of many abstract paintings) depends upon an even distribution of surface effects, so does the merit of a wallpaper lie in its 'all-over' repetitive quality. And it is only a repeated pattern which gains by repetition, that can do the various things such as fuse space, or play tricks with it—a good wallpaper ought to do.

1955 MICHAEL FARR. *Design in British Industry* (Cambridge University Press). Contains an informed and critical chapter on the wallpaper industry.

1955 JOHN E. BLAKE. *Design* (December). Illustrated article, entitled 'Designing Wallpapers'.

The aesthetic problem is the most complex and the least tangible, partly because the levels of taste which are catered for vary to an enormous extent, and partly because personal predilections about design are often irrational and intuitive. The general direction in which wallpaper design has been moving since the war is, however, clear. The introduction six or seven years ago of a few simple dot and stripe motifs in expensive hand printed ranges was the first sign that wallpapers could in fact contribute to a modern interior, and help banish the austerity of wartime life as Dior's 'New Look' had already attempted to do in another field.

This was commented upon in a *Manchester Guardian* leader (December 7)

1955 *A Century of British Fabrics, 1850-1950.* (F. Lewis, Ltd. The Tithe House, Leigh-on-Sea.) Section on Wallpaper. Illustrated.

As with all design forms there are many debased examples to be seen but the best of these new designs rely upon character of drawing, simplicity, texture and colour, and the limitless variety of ways in which they can be used together to create original schemes.

1955 DECORATED PAPERS. Notes on a display of decorated papers from the Collection of MRS. OLGA HIRSCH, 10 Adams Road, Cambridge, for the members of the Double Crown Club. June 23. References to wallpapers made by the Dominotiers of France, etc.

1956 Council of Industrial Design. International Design Congress, September 11-13. Among the many papers read during the Congress were two which dealt exclusively with wallpaper design. The first by Dr. Emil Rasch, Chairman and Managing Director of Tapetenfabrik Gebr. Rasch & Co., Germany; the second by E. A. Entwisle. All these papers summarised in C.O.I.D. publication, *The Management of Design.*

1956 *The Sphere* (November 9). Short Illustrated Article, 'The Art of Wallpaper' (anonymous).

1956 *The Furnishers' Encyclopaedia*, edited by MICHAEL SHERIDAN. (National Trade Press Ltd). Article on Wallpaper.

1956 DOREEN YARWOOD, *The English Home* (Batsford). A useful book on English Interior Decoration. Many notes on wallpaper.

1956 Wallpaper Exhibition at Foyles, Charing Cross Road, London. 'Three Centuries of Taste and Comment' (February). A number of articles on this exhibition appeared in the national press during this time, among them *Daily Express, Daily Mail, The Queen, Manchester Guardian, The Lady*, etc.

1956 ADA K. LONGFIELD (Mrs. H. G. Leask). *Country Life* (March 15). 'French Scenic Wallpapers'. A very accurate and scholarly article well worth recording for reference.

The distinctive feature of these papers was that they provided a continuous series of pictures, and since all parts depicted successive stages in a story, or different views in a panorama, they had to be made without any of the repetition of pattern common to ordinary wallpapers. The initial outlay for their production was consequently very high. Even apart from the expense of the working designs—for which French artists of note were usually employed—there was the cost of the 1,500, 2,000 or perhaps 3,000 separate blocks required for each set of ten, twelve, or sixteen large scenes. Finally the accurate handling of such quantities of material for the printing necessitated specially skilful workmanship and careful supervision.

1956 W. G. SUTHERLAND, *Manchester Guardian.* Supplement to the issue September 25. 'Diversity in Contemporary Wallpapers'.

1956 H. DALTON CLIFFORD, *Home Decorations.* A 'Homes and Gardens' Book published by *Country Life.*

Amusing patterns on wallpaper soon cease to amuse when one becomes familiar with them—it has to be a very good joke to stand constant repetition.

1956 ROSAMOND BAYNE-POWELL, *Housekeeping in the 18th Century.* (Murray). A few references relating to wallpaper (see II, Interior Decoration).

1956 JOHN BETJEMAN, *The Spectator* (September 7). 'Railway Sandwich de Luxe'.

A friend and I ordered two tongue sandwiches each and coffee for two in the King's Cross Hotel, London, which is run by British Railways. The bill was 15s. Is this one of the ways by which the unlucky Sir Brian Robertson is trying to make his railways pay? or are we paying for the 'contemporary' papers and paint with which that once noble hotel has been decorated.

1956 *Punch* (April 25). Satirical article on Contemporary Interior Decoration entitled 'A Popular Author at Home'. Fully illustrated.

1957 *Encyclopaedia of Antiques,* Vol. III (Connoisseur publication). Article on collecting old wallpaper by E. A. ENTWISLE. Illustrated.

Wallpaper is necessarily a somewhat ephemeral thing and we do well to prize the examples that come our way. Every additional discovery contributes to the history of the subject: from these we learn something of social conditions and taste throughout the centuries. The popularity of wallpaper has been increasing ever since it was first invented, and who knows, there may be a profitable side for the discerning connoisseur in collecting some of the finer types that are being produced to-day.

1957 *Apollo* (April). 'Panoramic Designs in Wallpaper', Anonymous. Illustrated. Reference to French designs.

1957 *The Scotsman* (March 6). 'Choosing a new Wallpaper'.

. . . If you want to bring the tropics into your living room you can have an exotic looking rubber plant running riot over your walls. Possibly to discourage any jungle wild life from paying you a visit the paper intended to be used in conjunction with this is designed like an unscalable bamboo fence, which should give adequate protection in any living room.

1957 TAPESTRY. See article in *Encyclopaedia Britannica* under this heading by PHYLLIS ACKERMAN. Illustrated. A very full and informative account of its history and technique.

1957 *Encyclopaedia Britannica.* Article on Wallpaper History, Design and Manufacture. By E. A. E. Illustrated.

1957 'MURAL PAINTING'. Article by GEORGE BIDDLE. *Encyclopaedia Britannica.* Illustrated. Bibliography.

1957 *Tit-Bits* (September 28).

A guest had been admiring the new wallpaper in his host's lounge, when the small son of the house strolled in and with a crayon drew a huge pink elephant all over the wall. 'I say,' exclaimed the startled visitor, 'did you see what your boy did?' 'Yes,' said the host proudly, 'and do you know, he's only seen an elephant once in his life.'

1957 MARGARET and ALEXANDER POTTER, *Interiors.* (John Murray). Illustrated. A record of some of the changes in interior design and furniture of the English home from mediaeval times to the present day.

Mid-Twentieth Century. Within these houses the idea of picking out individual walls for special decorative treatment has spread from sources of impeccable taste. Applied without restraint however, it has led to enormous muddle and confusion. Plain and patterned walls, blue walls, red walls, stone walls (real and artificial) jostle together with uninhibited freedom, . . . etc.

1957 ADA K. LONGFIELD (Mrs. H. G. Leask), *Journal of The Royal Society of Antiquaries of Ireland,* Vol. LXXXVII, Part II. 'Old Wallpapers in Ireland'. A continuation of this author's earlier and most informative papers.

1957 MICHAEL THOMAS, *The Queen* (June 25). 'Random Reflections'.

'DON'T DO IT.' And as the shades of evening fall he takes his scissors and paste and sets to work papering the spare room, each wall of which must have a different paper!

1958 *Interior Decoration. Its History and Practice.* An Encyclopaedia Britannica Ltd. publication. A very comprehensive book of reference to wallpaper.

1958 LILY HUTCHINSON, *Manchester Guardian* (January 24). Mainly for Women page. Article entitled 'Stripes and Flowers—Memories of Wallpaper'.

. . . I always loved flowers and used to delight in the beautiful natural floral designs. I remember wondering why sprays of purple laburnum were included in a design where all the other flowers were in natural colours. It was years later when I went to see a famous wistaria growing on the wall of an inn at Banbury that I found it was my old friend the purple laburnum. I had never seen this growing in the North-west.

1958 PETER FLOUD, *Penrose Annual,* Vol. 52, pp. 10–14. 'Wallpaper Designs of C. F. A. Voysey'. A critical and informed evaluation of this artist's work. Illustrated.

The characteristic which decisively sets Voysey apart from all his contemporaries, and justifies our regarding him as one of the most original of all pattern designers, is the way in which he manages to use natural objects as a basis for repeating patterns formed from the juxtaposition of rhythmically contrasted flat shapes.

1958 JEAN WELSH, *Paper Making and Paper Selling*, Vol. LXXVII, Spring number. 'The Romance of Wallpaper'.

1958 GABRIEL FAGU & J. BRAUDEY, *Le Papier Peint*. Chronique succinct de papier peint en France. (Paris: La Chambre Syndicale des Fabricants de Papiers Peints de France). Contains much interesting information, including sections on the history of wallpaper; manufacture; types of wallpaper described, actual samples and ideas for the use of wallpapers in interior decoration; also dimensions of wallpaper and methods of paperhanging. A very complete list of French stockists, retailers, etc.

1958 Council of Industrial Design, *Designs of the Year 1958 and 1957*. Report of the Adjudicating Panels. Illustrated. See references to winning wallpaper designs, pp. 27 and 44, and many other C.O.I.D. publications in which the subject of wallpaper is touched upon.

1958 *Time and Tide* (August 2). 'Designs for Living'.

It is a safe guess that not one in fifty of those who throng the handsome wallpaper and fabric showrooms of Arthur Sanderson and Sons in Berner's Street, or in Glasgow, or the many Crown wallpaper shops could name the Company which controls them . . . the parent concern is the mighty Wall Paper Manufacturers Limited,' etc. . . .

1958 *Manchester Guardian*, 'Miscellany', September 16. Reference to a Do-it-Yourself Demonstration at Olympia:

. . . The finale was an exciting mugs-from-the-audience act which of course never fails. They enticed the young and the aged to prove that with a little tuition we can all plaster, paint and paper without embarrassment. It was a glorious opportunity for slap-stick. But the little boy did not fall into the paint and grandfather felt no urge to tip a bucket of paste over the lecturer or biff the smart young lady with a roll of paper. . . . It was a very typical scene of the late fifties. It ought to have been filmed and in years to come fitted into some pictorial social history of our times.

1958 WYNDHAM GOODDEN, *Design* (October). 'Problems for a Pace-setter'. A critical assessment of a new collection of 'Palladio' wallpapers.

1958 *Tapeten Zeitung* (Journal of the German wallpaper industry) (October).

France, England and America already possess standard works on wallpaper. It seems now that the ten-year-old project of producing a comprehensive German work on the subject is nearing its realization. It is on this account gratifying that the German manufacturers' Association have decided to finance such a book. Dr. Heinrich Olligs of Flammersheim & Steinmann, Cologne, has been entrusted with this work the preliminary planning for which is already in hand.

1958 WYNDHAM GOODDEN, *The Scotsman* (November 27). 'Textiles and Wallpapers'.

. . . A textile or a paper by itself is like a girl without a home. What will she become—a slut, a shrew, a saint, a politician, a madonna, or a cook? Until a piece of stuff, or piece of paper is chosen, cut into this or that proportion, set in such and such a room, lit by what lights, influenced by what colours, adjacent to what ornaments, etc., it hardly exists by itself at all.

1959 E. A. ENTWISLE, *The Connoisseur* (March). '18th Century London Paper-stainers. The Eckhardt Brothers of Chelsea'. Illustrated.

1959 *Investors' Chronicle* (May 1), p. 352. 'Wallpaper's Prosperity'. Well-informed article on the scope and prospects of the largest firm of wall-paper manufacturers in this country.

1959 PETER FLOUD, *Architectural Review* (July). 'Dating Morris Patterns'. Investigation into the sources of inspiration of Morris's designs for wall-papers, etc. Illustrated.

1959 PAPER MAKING. RUPERT C. JARVIS, *The Paper-Makers and the Excise in the Eighteenth Century*. The Library, Fifth Series, Vol. XIV, No. 2 (June). A paper read before the Bibliographical Society, November 19, 1957. Includes interesting sidelights on the duties imposed con-currently on 'paper; printed, painted or stained', i.e. wallpaper.

1959 *Les Beaux Arts* (Brussels) (May 29). 'Le Papier, revêtement mural, jadis, aujourd'hui et demain', by 'A.S.'

1959 *Interiors* (U.S.A.) (November). 'In Memory of a Pioneer—Nancy Vincent McClelland 1877–1959.' Biographical details of the career of this great American authority on wallpaper.

1959 ALFRED WHITTLE, F.C.A., *Stock Exchange Gazette* (December 11). 'How I read the Future for Wallpaper'. 'Consumption is probably now running between 115 and 120 million rolls a year but the quality is going up all the time in response to public demand.

1960 MURAL PAINTING. EDWARD CROFT-MURRAY, 'Decorative Painting in England 1537–1837. (*Country Life*.) To be published during 1960.

1960 SACHEVERELL SITWELL, in an article contributed to the privately printed brochure *A Century of Sanderson—1860–1960*.

> *It is only a pity there are no black and white pictorial wallpapers by Aubrey Beardsley who in his tragically short life adapted his art with such skill and instinct to the prosaic needs of the process block, and might have designed paperhangings such as have never been before or since. A number of contemporary painters and designers have been given their opportunity since then so that it could be said with truth that the craft of wallpaper is in more flourishing condition than ever.*

1960 International Wallpaper Congress (I.C.I.) Munich. 23–27 April. Catalogue of the Wallpaper Exhibition designed by Gunter Hennig. Fully illustrated with current examples of European wallpapers, bibliography, etc.

Extract from introductory comments by Walter Gropius.

> *Wallpaper of a high order, both in quality and taste, is a main ally of the individual inhabitant. It enables him to achieve outstanding room effects by simple means and to vary these within a given frame by wise selection, depending on the changing requirements of his life.*

INDEX

Numerals in **heavy type** refer to the figure numbers of the illustrations. In some cases references are to items which occur more than once on a page